Fagatele Bay National Marine Sanctuary

CONDITION REPORT 2007

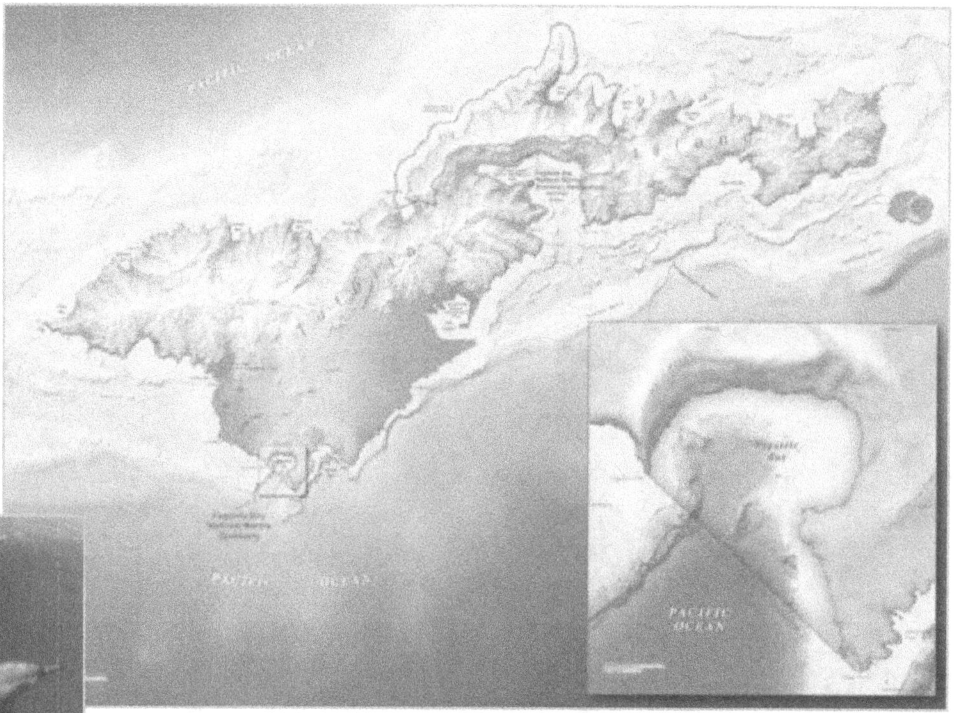

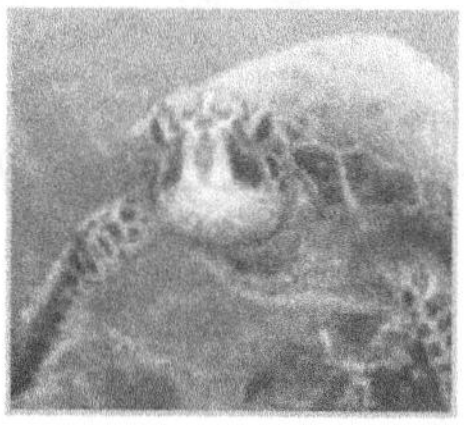

I0413099

NATIONAL MARINE SANCTUARIES

noaa

August 2007

U.S. Department of Commerce
Carlos M. Gutierrez, Secretary

National Oceanic and Atmospheric Administration
VADM Conrad C. Lautenbacher, Jr. (USN-ret.)
Under Secretary of Commerce for Oceans
and Atmosphere

National Ocean Service
John H. Dunnigan, Assistant Administrator

National Marine Sanctuary Program
Daniel J. Basta, Director

National Oceanic and Atmospheric Administration
National Marine Sanctuary Program
SSMC4, N/ORM62
1305 East-West Highway
Silver Spring, MD 20910
301-713-3125
http://sanctuaries.noaa.gov/

Fagatele Bay National Marine Sanctuary
PO Box 4318
Pago Pago, American Samoa 96799
684-633-7354
http://fagatelebay.noaa.gov/

American Samoa Government
Tagiola T.A. Tulafono, Governor

American Samoa Department of Commerce
Faleseu Eliu Paopao, Director

Report Preparation:

National Marine Sanctuary Program:
Kathy Broughton, Stephen R. Gittings

Fagatele Bay National Marine Sanctuary:
William Kiene

Clancy Environmental Consultants, Inc.:
Karen Fox, Jeffrey Rosen
http://clancyenv.com

Copy Editor: Matt Dozier

Graphic Designer: Auralea Krieger

Cover photo credits counterclockwise from top left:

Children: Kip Evans, Dolphins: Ed Lyman, Whale Tail: NOAA, Fagatele Bay Cliffs: Kip Evans, Clown Fish: NOAA, Green Sea Turtle: Claire Johnson, Coral and Fish: Nancy Daschbach, Map: Produced by the National Marine Sanctuary Program. The bathymetric data shown on this map is derived from many disparate multibeam cruise missions and have been merged together in a GIS to create a single data grid for display purposes only. This map should not be used for scientific or navigational purposes. Shallow Water Bathymetric Data to -250 meters: The Coral Reef Ecosystem Divison of NOAA's Pacific Islands Fisheries Science Center with funding from NOAA's Coral Reef Conservation Program. Data and metadata available from: http://www.soest.hawaii.edu/pibhmc/ pibhmc_AmSamoa.htm; Deep Water Bathymetric Data: Brian Donahue, Univ. S. Fl. Jan 2002. SimRAD EM-120 Multibeam Bathymetry Grid, Tutuila Flanks, American Samoa. Metadata available from: http://dusk. geo.orst.edu/djl/samoa/data/revelle.htm; Scripps Institute of Ocean- ography, UCSD – multiple cruise datasets. Available from: http://nsdl. sdsc.edu/tools.html.

Suggested Citation:

National Marine Sanctuary Program. 2007. Fagatele Bay National Ma- rine Sanctuary Condition Report 2007. U.S. Department of Commerce, National Oceanic and Atmospheric Administration, National Marine Sanctuary Program, Silver Spring, MD. 39 pp.

Table of Contents

Abstract

Fagatele Bay is an isolated national marine sanctuary contained within a small, flooded volcanic crater on the southern coast of Tutuila, American Samoa. The site is uniquely rich in both natural resources and cultural heritage. Fagatele Bay and its fringing coral reef have experienced severe disruptions from cyclones, crown-of-thorns starfish outbreaks, and more recently from coral bleaching and diseases (the causes of these are not fully understood). However, recovery has been remarkably swift in comparison to other coral reef ecosystems, and the bay's isolation from most direct human influences has kept it relatively unspoiled. The most significant threats to the reef from human activities include over-fishing, poaching (especially by blast-fishing and spearfishing at night), and land clearing for agricultural development. There are also concerns about the increasing visitors as tourism increases in American Samoa.

By most measures, water quality in Fagatele Bay appears to be relatively good, but observations suggest declining conditions. The frequency of coral bleaching has increased in recent years, owing to higher water temperature. Nutrient levels and sediment loads, while not yet known to be a problem, are likely to increase with land clearing on the steep slopes that surround the small bay. These influences could reduce the resistance of living resources to diseases and bleaching and promote fleshy algal growth on the reef. Habitat quality is fairly good, as indicated by resilient coral populations and high diversity; however, destructive fishing activities (particularly blast fishing,) have harmed some areas of the reef. Certain indicators of living resource quality, namely diversity, reef coral recruitment and growth, and the lack of invasive species, suggest good conditions. Other indicators, most notably the lack of large predatory fish, clearly reflect the influence of fishing and selective fishing practices. Of concern to resource managers are the potential negative effects this may have on non-targeted fish species, benthic invertebrates and algae growth. These have been documented elsewhere when food webs have been disrupted and include algal blooms, species extirpations and invasions, and changes in dominance patterns.

Fagatele Bay National Marine Sanctuary

- *Located at the southern tip of the island of Tutuila, American Samoa*
- *0.25 square miles, the smallest of the national marine sanctuaries*
- *Flooded crater of an extinct volcano*
- *Congressionally designated in 1986 as a national marine sanctuary*
- *Administered jointly by NOAA and the American Samoa Department of Commerce*
- *Extremely diverse and prolific fringing coral reef ecosystem*
- *Threatened by storm damage, coral bleaching, coral and coralline algae diseases, and destructive fishing*
- *Highly resilient ecosystem, which has recovered from numerous natural and human induced disruptions that have occurred over the last three decades*

The staff at the Fagatele Bay sanctuary and territorial partners already work together on management, research, monitoring, education and outreach. Coordinating with American Samoa's Coral Reef Advisory Group, action plans are in place to deal with a number of the threats to Samoan reefs, including fishing, climate change, land-based pollution and population pressure. Fagatele Bay sanctuary staff are working with staff at the American Samoa Environmental Protection Agency to improve water quality monitoring in the bay, particularly with respect to bacteria levels and land development. The sanctuary program will work with the U.S. Geological Survey to assess threats posed by a nearby landfill facility. Mooring buoy installations are expected to reduce threats to habitat from anchoring, but enforcement will have to be improved to reduce damage caused by illegal fishing. Continuation of the long-term monitoring program in the bay is considered a top priority for Fagatele Bay sanctuary and will allow management to gauge long-term patterns of change and recovery.

The unique Polynesian culture of the people of American Samoa has tools that can teach environmental stewardship not only to the local population, but also to the world. Sanctuary staff are looking to the relationships of the Samoan culture to the land and sea to help guide the future of resource protection in Fagatele Bay National Marine Sanctuary.

Fagatele Bay National Marine Sanctuary
Condition Summary Table

Condition Summary: The results in the following table are a compilation of findings from the "State of Sanctuary Resources" section of this report. (For further clarification of the questions posed in the table, see Appendix A.)

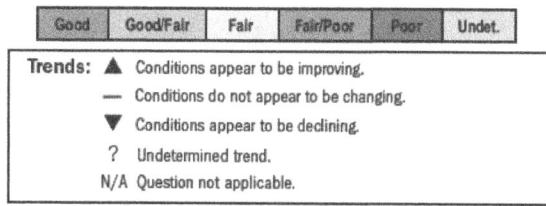

| Good | Good/Fair | Fair | Fair/Poor | Poor | Undet. |

Trends: ▲ Conditions appear to be improving.
— Conditions do not appear to be changing.
▼ Conditions appear to be declining.
? Undetermined trend.
N/A Question not applicable.

#	Questions/Resources	Rating	Basis for Judgment	Description of Findings	Sanctuary Response
WATER					
1	Are specific or multiple stressors, including changing oceanographic and atmospheric conditions, affecting water quality and how are they changing?	▼	Increasing number of warm-water events causing coral bleaching	Selected conditions may inhibit the development of assemblages, and may cause measurable but not severe declines in living resources and habitats.	American Samoa and sanctuary regulations have been designed to prevent any reduction in water quality. *Enterococcus* bacterial concentrations are measured to assess how land development affects water quality. Staff are also proposing to assess the groundwater beneath the island landfill to determine if contaminants are being transported into the marine environment (page 20).
2	What is the eutrophic condition of sanctuary waters and how is it changing?	—	Low nutrient levels, good water clarity; lack of fleshy algae	Conditions do not appear to have the potential to negatively affect living resources or habitat quality.	
3	Do sanctuary waters pose risks to human health and how are they changing?	?	No known risks	Conditions do not appear to have the potential to negatively affect human health.	
4	What are the levels of human activities that may influence water quality and how are they changing?	▼	Land clearing for agriculture, proximity of island landfill	Some potentially harmful activities exist, but they do not appear to have had a negative effect on water quality.	
HABITAT					
5	What are the abundance and distribution of major habitat types and how are they changing?	?	Resilient coral populations; destructive fishing activities, diseases present	Selected habitat loss or alteration has taken place, precluding full development of living resource assemblages, but it is unlikely to cause substantial or persistent degradation in living resources or water quality.	Regulations prohibit destructive activities, such as fishing and anchoring, that disturb or damage natural features. Mooring buoys were installed in 2006 to eliminate the need for anchoring (page 20).
6	What is the condition of biologically structured habitats and how is it changing?	—	Destructive events have not reduced biodiversity	Selected habitat loss or alteration has taken place, precluding full development of living resources, but it is unlikely to cause substantial or persistent degradation in living resources or water quality.	
7	What are the contaminant concentrations in sanctuary habitats and how are they changing?	—	None identified	Contaminants do not appear to have the potential to negatively affect living resources or water quality.	
8	What are the levels of human activities that may influence habitat quality and how are they changing?	—	Low visitation, but fishing impacts occur	Some potentially harmful activities exist, but they do not appear to have had a negative effect on habitat quality.	
LIVING RESOURCES					
9	What is the status of biodiversity and how is it changing?	—	All species present, but some in low numbers	Biodiversity appears to reflect pristine or near-pristine conditions and promotes ecosystem integrity (full community development and function).	Regulations prohibit removing or disturbing marine invertebrates or plants. Most fishing gears are excluded from the sanctuary. Regulations by federal and state partners protect marine mammals, birds, and sea turtles from "take," disturbance and harm. Field assessments of coral and fish populations, coral diseases and other indicators of coral reef health are conducted (pages 20 - 21).
10	What is the status of environmentally sustainable fishing and how is it changing?	—	Fishing has removed large fish	Extraction has caused or is likely to cause severe declines in some but not all ecosystem components and reduce ecosystem integrity.	
11	What is the status of non-indigenous species and how is it changing?	—	Some non-indigenous algae and invertebrates may be present	Non-indigenous species are not suspected or do not appear to affect ecosystem integrity (full community development and function).	
12	What is the status of key species and how is it changing?	—	Reduced numbers and size of certain predatory fish species	The reduced abundance of selected keystone species has caused or is likely to cause severe declines in some but not all ecosystem components, and reduce ecosystem integrity; or selected key species are at substantially reduced levels, and prospects for recovery are uncertain.	
13	What is the condition or health of key species and how is it changing?	▼	Coral and coralline algae diseases	The condition of selected key resources is not optimal, perhaps precluding full ecological function, but substantial or persistent declines are not expected.	
14	What are the levels of human activities that may influence living resource quality and how are they changing?	?	Illegal and legal fishing continues to remove large fish	Selected activities have caused or are likely to cause severe impacts, and cases to date suggest a pervasive problem.	
MARITIME ARCHAEOLOGICAL RESOURCES					
15	What is the integrity of known maritime archaeological resources and how is it changing?	N/A	No documented underwater archeological sites	N/A	Although no maritime archaeological artifacts have been identified in the sanctuary, regulations prohibit the removal, damage or disturbance of any historical or cultural resource within the sanctuary (page 21).
16	Do known maritime archaeological resources pose an environmental hazard and is this threat changing?	N/A	No documented underwater archeological sites	N/A	
17	What are the levels of human activities that may influence maritime archaeological resource quality and how are they changing?	N/A	No documented underwater archeological sites	N/A	

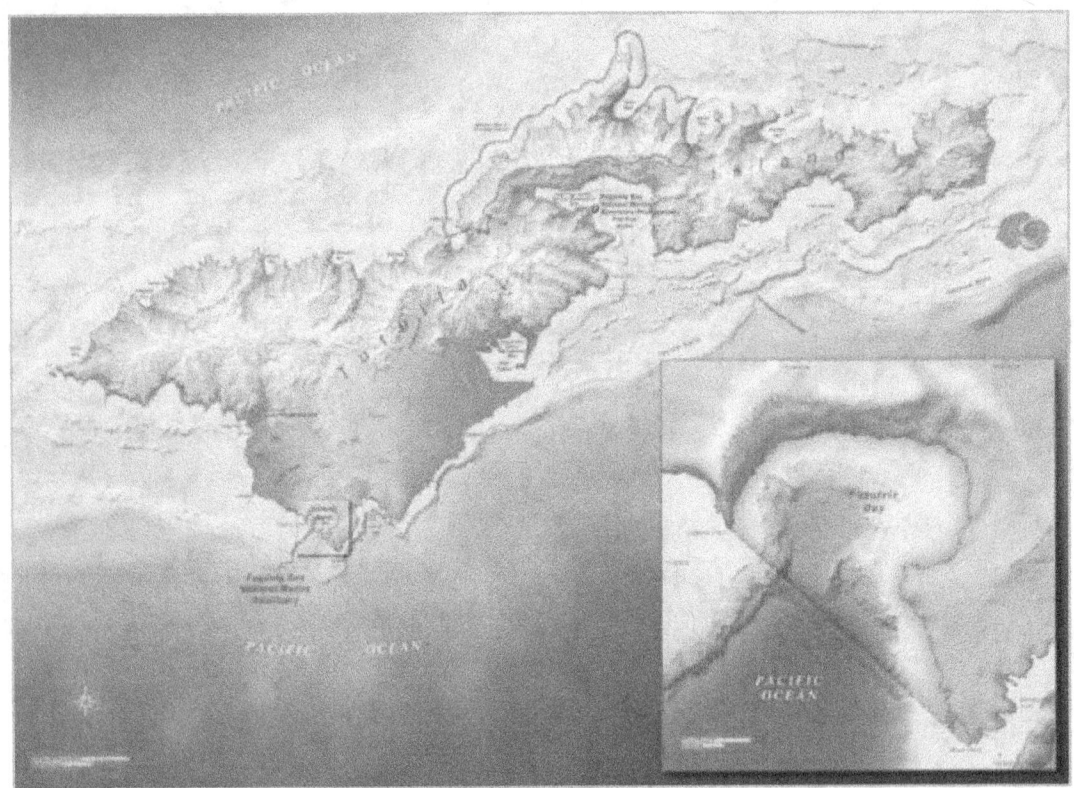

NATIONAL MARINE
SANCTUARIES

FAGATELE BAY

About This Report

This report provides a summary of resources in the National Oceanic and Atmospheric Administration's Fagatele Bay National Marine Sanctuary, pressures on those resources, the current condition and trends, and management responses to the pressures that threaten the integrity of the marine environment. Specifically, this document includes information on the status and trends of water quality, habitat, living resources and maritime archaeological resources and the human activities that affect them. It presents responses to a set of questions posed to all sanctuaries (Appendix A). Resource status is rated on a scale from good to poor, and the timelines used for comparison vary from topic to topic. Trends in the status of resources are also reported, and are generally based on observed changes in status over the past five years, unless otherwise specified. Evaluations of status and trends were made by sanctuary staff, based on interpretation of quantitative and, when necessary, non-quantitative assessments and observations of scientists, managers and users. In many cases, sanctuary staff

consulted outside experts familiar with the resources and with knowledge of previous and current scientific investigations. The ratings reflect the collective interpretation of the status of local issues of concern among sanctuary program staff and outside experts based on their knowledge and perceptions of local problems, but the final ratings were determined by sanctuary staff. Similar reports summarizing resource status and trends will be prepared for each marine sanctuary approximately every five years and updated as new information allows. This information is intended to help set the stage for management plan reviews at each site and to help sanctuary staff identify monitoring, characterization and research priorities to address gaps, day-to-day information needs and new threats. This report has been peer-reviewed and complies with the White House Office of Management and Budget's peer review standards as outlined in the Final Information Quality Bulletin for Peer Review.

Introduction

The National Marine Sanctuary Program manages marine areas in both nearshore and open ocean waters that range in size from less than one to almost 140,000 square miles. Each area has its own concerns and requirements for environmental monitoring. Nevertheless, ecosystem structure and function in all these areas have similarities and are influenced by common factors that interact in comparable ways. Furthermore, the human influences that affect the structure and function of these sites are similar in a number of ways. For these reasons, in 2001 the program began to implement System-Wide Monitoring (SWiM). The monitoring framework (National Marine Sanctuary Program, 2004) facilitates the development of effective, ecosystem-based monitoring programs that address management information needs using a design process that can be applied in a consistent way at multiple spatial scales and to multiple resource types. It identifies four primary components common among marine ecosystems: water, habitats, living resources, and maritime archaeological resources.

By assuming that a common marine ecosystem framework can be applied to all places, the National Marine Sanctuary Program developed a series of questions that are posed to every sanctuary and used as evaluation criteria to assess resource condition and trends. The questions, which are shown on page iii and explained in Appendix A, are derived from both a generalized ecosystem framework and from the National Marine Sanctuary Program's mission. They are widely applicable across the system of areas managed by the sanctuary program and provide a tool with which the program can measure its progress in maintaining and improving natural and archaeological resource quality throughout the system.

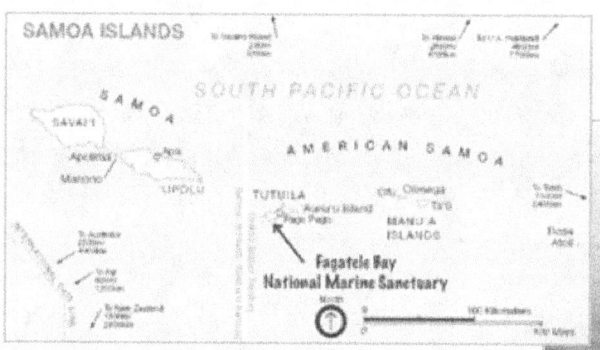

American Samoa is a group of islands located in the South Pacific Ocean, about halfway between Hawai'i and New Zealand.

The Fagatele Bay sanctuary is located at the southern-most point of Tutuila Island, American Samoa.

Fagatele Bay is surrounded by 200-400 foot cliffs and steep slopes covered with dense, lush vegetation.

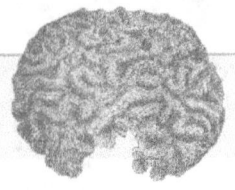

Site History and Resources

Overview

Fagatele Bay is the smallest and most remote of the national marine sanctuaries, but its coral reefs may have the highest marine life diversity in the sanctuary system. The bay's habitats are home to a variety of tropical fish, invertebrates and algae. Fagatele Bay sanctuary was designated as a national marine sanctuary in 1986 because it serves as an extraordinary example of a tropical marine environment and coral reef ecosystem of exceptional productivity. The sanctuary is co-administered by the National Oceanic and Atmospheric Administration (NOAA), within the U.S. Department of Commerce, and the American Samoa Department of Commerce.

Located in the South Pacific Ocean along the southern coast of American Samoa's main island of Tutuila, the Fagatele Bay sanctuary protects a one-quarter square mile (163-acre) marine area. With water visibility normally around 20-30 meters (65-98 feet), the small bay is a partially drowned crater of an extinct volcano and is bordered by a ridge 60-120 meters (200-400 feet) high with vertical cliffs and steep slopes. These slopes are covered with dense, lush vegetation composing one of America's few tropical rainforests. The steepness of the ridges surrounding Fagatele Bay has helped ensure that most of the watershed has remained free of introduced vegetation, maintaining a relatively unspoiled refuge for American Samoa's native plants and wildlife.

Fagatele Bay sanctuary's marine environment is typical of the fringing coral reef ecosystems associated with high islands of volcanic origin, many of which lie in the warm waters of the Pacific Ocean. Coral reefs are key coastal marine ecosystems in the tropical Pacific and provide vital coastal protection and marine resource utilization by the people who live in the region. Fagatele Bay National Marine Sanctuary was designated to help preserve American Samoa's coastal resources and to contribute to coral reef conservation efforts throughout the Pacific.

Due to the need to protect the natural resources represented by Fagatele Bay and the need to enhance public awareness of marine resource protection and marine ecosystem research, the

Humpback whale. *Photo: Josh Pederson*

governor of American Samoa proposed Fagatele Bay to NOAA as a candidate for marine sanctuary designation in 1982. After a lengthy period of public hearings, consultation and review, a management plan was approved, culminating in the designation of the sanctuary on April 29, 1986 by an act of Congress. The Fagatele Bay sanctuary is part of American Samoa's conservation strategy, which includes the National Park of American Samoa and a community-based marine protected area program coordinated by the Department of Marine and Wildlife Resources.

Location

Fagatele Bay lies along the southernmost shore of Tutuila, the largest and most populated of the seven islands comprising the U.S. Territory of American Samoa. Tutuila is the center of all administrative and economic activity, and home to over 90 percent of American Samoa's population of 65,500. Annual population growth is currently high at around 2 percent and the population is predicted to exceed 76,000 people by 2020. Located approximately 1,600 kilometers south of the equator, American Samoa constitutes the eastern portion of the Samoan archipelago. The islands of Savai'i and Upolu to the west form the independent nation of Samoa. American Samoa is the only U.S. Territory south of the equator and comprises five volcanic islands (Tutuila, Aunuu, Ofu, Olosega, and Tau) and two small remote coral atolls (Rose Atoll and Swains Island).

Geology

Tutuila Island is composed of Pliocene or early Pleistocene volcanics extruded approximately 1.5 million years ago by a series of volcanic eruptions. The island consists primarily of basaltic rocks, with the bulk of the island being made up of lava flows. Because of rapid submergence during the last period of Pleistocene sea level rise, the fringing reefs around Tutuila are discontinuous and have their foundation on bedded calcareous sand and silt as well as coral reef limestone deposited over the last 10,000 years.

Tutuila lies on the Pacific Plate, which moves in a westward direction at about 7 centimeters (3 inches) per year. Approximately 160 kilometers south of the island, the Pacific Plate collides with the Australian Plate, causing the Pacific Plate to slowly break into two parts. As the northern section of the plate continues to move westward, the southern section slides beneath the Australian Plate, forming the 10-kilometer-deep Tongan Trench. The Samoan archipelago rides on this northern section of the Pacific Plate. The islands formed as the plate traveled over a "hot spot" of volcanic activity. As a consequence, the islands of American Samoa are geologically younger than Savai'i and Upolou, the islands of Independent Samoa to the west. The "hot spot" is presently located 50 kilometers east of Ta'u Island, where ongoing volcanic eruptions on the seafloor are building a new island (Vailulu'u) that has yet to rise above the sea surface.

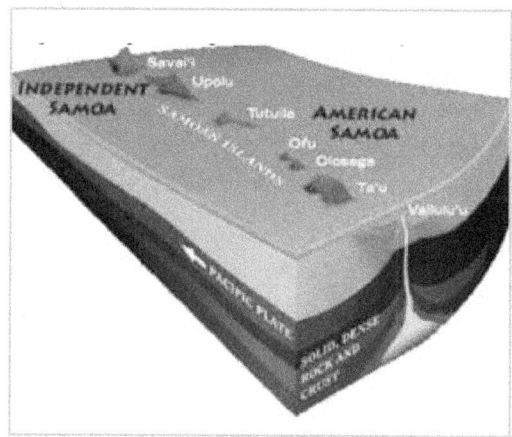

The Samoan archipelago was formed by volcanic eruptions from a hot spot beneath the seafloor. These eruptions accumulated lava on the seafloor until it emerged above sea level and formed islands. As the Pacific crust moved west over this hot spot, the eruptions created the islands that make up the independent nation of Samoa and American Samoa. American Samoa is younger than its western neighbor. The hot spot is actively extruding new lava east of Ta'u that may eventually reach sea level and form a new island. Image: Jayne Doucette, WHOI

Diver above some plate coral, *Acorpora hycinthus*. Photo: Kip Evans   Sea Star.

Human Settlement

Archeological evidence suggests the islands of Samoa have been inhabited since at least 1300 B.C. While trade and social interactions with Tonga and the other islands of the Pacific occurred over the subsequent 2,000 years, a distinctly Samoan society existed in the islands by the time of European arrival. Jacob Roggeveen first documented the islands in 1722, but Louis de Bougainville's 1772 name for the archipelago, the "Navigator Islands," was used until the end of the 19th century. La Peróuse was the first European to set foot on Tutuila in 1787. The Wilkes Expedition from the U.S. in 1837 provided the first systematic natural history and cultural surveys of Samoa. This expedition and the arrival of Christian missionaries established the Western influence over Samoan society that continues today. Although the shore of Fagatele Bay was the site of a village from prehistoric times to the 1950s, at present no settlement exists in the sanctuary other than a simple structure housing two temporary agricultural workers.

Commerce

In 1878, the U.S. Navy established a lease of land on the shore of the deep harbor at Pago Pago at Tutuila for a coaling station. The subsequent relationship between American Samoa and the United States has brought dramatic changes to the territory's economy. Despite significant social, economic and religious change, Samoan cultural traditions remain strong in American Samoa society, governance and land tenure. Today, tuna processing and the territorial government are the largest employers and the mainstay of the territory's economy. Two large U.S. tuna canneries form the basis of an industry that employs more than 3,000 Samoan and foreign workers. International fishing fleets supply catches to the canneries for export while small-scale artisanal fisheries supply the local market for fish. Tuna canned in South America, which is allowed into the U.S. duty-free under the Andean Trade Preferences Act, threatens the future viability of the tuna industry in American Samoa.

Retail trade and services dominate the rest of the territory's economy. Agriculture on the islands of American Samoa mainly supplies local markets. The most important crops include taro, coconuts, bananas, oranges, pineapples, papayas, breadfruit, and yams. Tourism is not well developed in American Samoa, but short visits by cruise ships are a periodic addition to the economy.

Climate and Water Quality

Yearly air temperatures in American Samoa range from 21 to 32 °C (70 to 90 °F), with an average humidity of 80 percent. The average yearly rainfall is about 5 meters (200 inches), with the heaviest rains occurring during summer months, from December through March. As summer progresses, the temperature of the ocean's surface waters also increases by about 3 °C (6 °F). Warmer ocean temperatures, in turn, help provide the energy to start tropical cyclones. Thus, the chance of a cyclone is greatest between November and April. The mean annual water temperature of Fagatele Bay fluctuates around 28 °C (82 °F).

Habitat

Fagatele Bay formed when the seaward side of the Fagatele volcanic crater was breached by the ocean and flooded sometime in the Pleistocene. The resulting geography is a well-protected marine environment recessed into the adjoining land and surrounded by steep-sided ridges. Seumalo Ridge rises over 120 meters (400 feet) high along the western and northern sides of Fagatele Bay, while the eastern side of the bay is bounded by Manautuloa Ridge at over 60 meters (200 feet) high. Although foot trails exist to lead hikers from the mountain ridge to the shore, the steepness of the slope makes access to the bay from land difficult.

The prevalent feature of Fagatele Bay sanctuary is its extensive coral reef ecosystem. Shallow-water coral reefs and reef-building organisms are confined to the upper euphotic zone, with the majority of reef production occurring in less than 10 meters (33 feet) of water. Maximum water depth in Fagatele Bay National

Aerial image of Fagatele Bay showing shallow coral reefs and deep (dark blue) water habitats. Line A-B marks location of cross-section shown on following page. Photo: USDA, 1991.

Marine Sanctuary is 170 meters (560 feet), with open ocean depths to the southwest dropping off steeply to more than 1,200 meters (4,000 feet). Due to the excellent water and habitat conditions found in Fagatele Bay, corals are capable of thriving to depths of more than 30 meters (90 feet).

Fagatele Bay's coral reef consists of a near-shore inner reef flat that slopes to a deeper water reef (reef slope) farther offshore. The reef crest, between the inner reef flat and outer reef slope, lies in extremely shallow water and is exposed during the lowest tides.

Waves commonly break on the reef crest. The fringing reefs found in Fagatele Bay, and their geographic orientation relative to prevailing winds, moderates shoreline erosion from ocean waves.

Living Resources

The coral reefs of Fagatele Bay provide habitat for at least 271 species of fishes. Abundant groups include adult and juvenile damselfish, surgeonfish, wrasse, butterflyfish, and parrotfish. Surveys have also identified 200 species of coral living on the

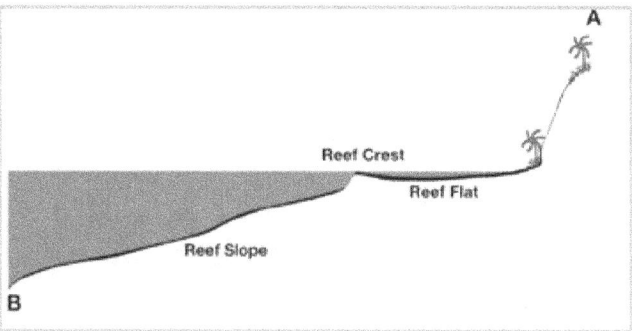

A cross-section of Fagatele Bay's fringing reef at line A-B shown in photo on previous page. The shallow reef flat and crest is often exposed on low tides and the reef slope descends to water depths of 170 meters (560 feet). *Source: Bill Kiene*

reefs in the sanctuary. Corals play a particularly important role in coral reef ecosystems because they provide shelter and habitat for the abundant varieties of marine life that make coral reefs their home. Many species on coral reefs depend on one another in various ways. For example, some damselfish and corals have a symbiotic relationship. The corals' branches provide the fish with protection from predators, and the fish excrete nitrogen in the form of ammonia, which the corals use for growth. Throughout the reef ecosystem, close, complex relationships like this exist between very different types of organisms, creating an extremely diverse and highly productive biological community. Sponge, mollusk,

echinoderm, crustacean, annelid, bryozoan and tunicate fauna are integral components of the overall biodiversity. Taxonomic surveys have identified at least 1,400 species of algae and invertebrates (other than coral) living on Tutuila's coral reefs and likely to be found in Fagatele Bay.

In addition to fishes and invertebrate coral reef organisms, several species of dolphin (e.g., Pacific bottlenose and spinner dolphin) are found in the vicinity of the Fagatele Bay sanctuary. Hawksbill and green sea turtles are also frequently seen swimming in the bay.

The migratory paths of humpback whales in the southern hemisphere intersect with American Samoa. Each year, from July through October, humpbacks use the waters around American Samoa for breeding and calving. Occasionally, sperm whales venture into the waters surrounding American Samoa and may be seen seaward of Fagatele Bay.

Birds are the most conspicuous wildlife in American Samoa. 60 species have been documented by the U.S. Fish and Wildlife Service, of which 24 are seabirds and 36 are waterfowl. Eight of these species are introduced (in comparison, at least 142 species of birds from six continents have been introduced since

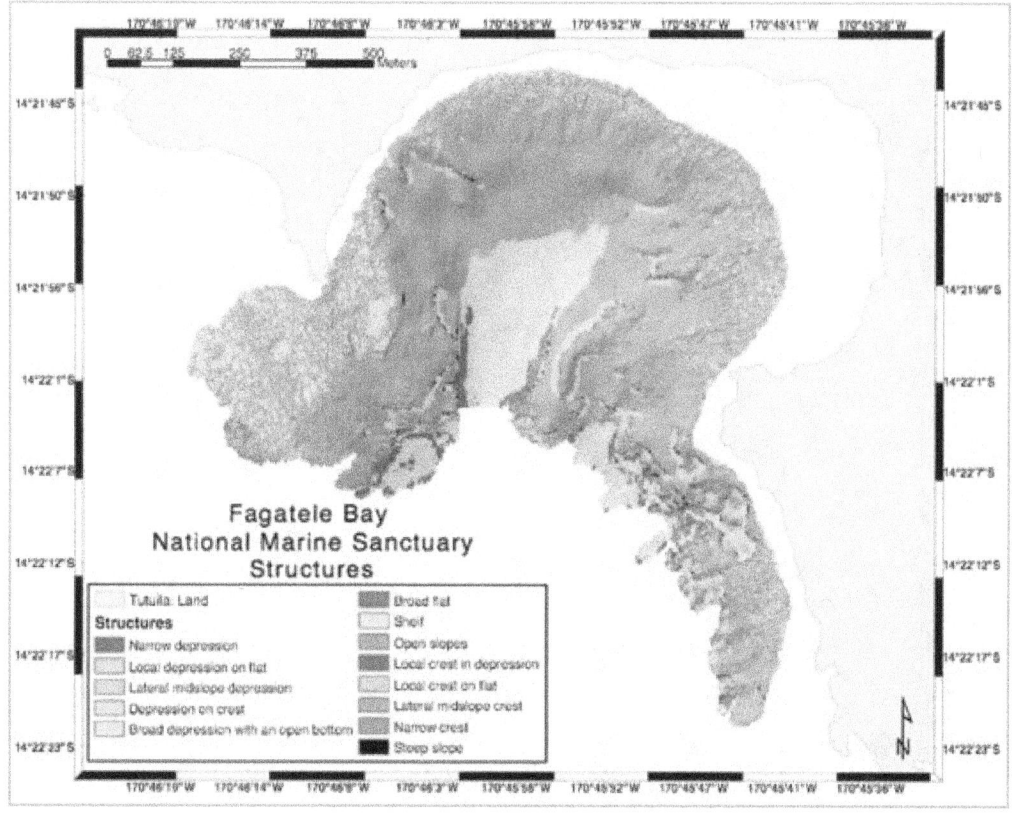

Map of the physical structures on the deep reef slopes within Fagatele Bay National Marine Sanctuary. These features are formed by the coral reefs and the sediments they produce. These structures have been deposited on top of the submerged geological features of the island. *Source: Fagatele Bay National Marine Sanctuary GIS Data Archive.*

Left image: The rich diversity of coral species and growth-forms in Fagatele Bay sanctuary create a multitude of complex habitats that are colonized by a variety of fish, algae and invertebrate life. This habitat complexity is what fuels the great biodiversity found on coral reefs. *Photo: Bill Kiene*
Right image: Whales are seen outside the Fagatele Bay sanctuary from July to October. *Photo: David Mattila*

1850 to the Hawaiian Islands (Moulton et al. 2001)). Birds use the shore, rocky cliffs and the surrounding heavily forested ridges for nesting and feeding. The area around the bay provides sea and shorebirds with comparatively remote, favorable physical environments for nesting, as well as ready access to rich foraging areas that are necessary during the breeding season. In addition to birds, large colonies of fruit bats, also known as flying foxes, reside in the forest surrounding Fagatele Bay. These bat colonies are infrequently encountered in other locations on Tutuila and are susceptible to human disturbance. The Fagatele Bay colonies are therefore important because of their relative isolation.

This clownfish and sea anemone live together in a mutually beneficial symbiotic relationship. The clownfish's waste provides the anemone nutrients, and the anemone protects the fish and its offspring from predators with its nematocysts (stinging cells). The fish has a protective coating that mimics the coating of the anemone and avoids its sting. *Photo: Kip Evans*

Maritime Archaeological Resources

Imagery and documentation of Fagatele Bay suggests that the sanctuary contains no large submerged archaeological artifacts. However, the site of at least one pre-historic village has been identified and mapped along its shore. This village site is presumed to be a long-occupied fishing village, which exploited the rich resources of the bay. The site consists of foundations of structures and pathways. The site is overgrown by thick forest vegetation and has not been excavated.

Pressures on the Sanctuary

Overview

The coral reefs of Fagatele Bay are resilient. They have been subjected to numerous impacts, but their ecological components have been quick to recover. This inherent resilience is an important consideration in the management of the sanctuary and to the understanding how coral reefs respond to disturbances.

Crown-of-Thorns Starfish Outbreak

The "crown-of-thorns" starfish, *Acanthaster planci* (alamea in the Samoan language), preys on coral. Usually, these starfish are a rare member of the reef community, however, plagues of "crown-of-thorns" starfish can occur for reasons that are not completely known. Such population outbreaks can rapidly kill large tracts of coral.

In 1978 and 1979, an outbreak of crown-of-thorns starfish devastated coral populations on Tutuila's reefs. The massive infestation resulted in a loss of more than 90 percent of all the living corals in Fagatele Bay. At the time, Fagatele Bay was not a

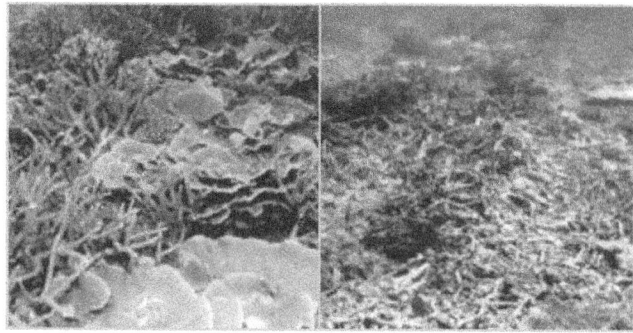

Left Image: Healthy coral communities in Fagatele Bay in 2006. *Photo: Richard Murphy* Right Image: Recently damaged and dead coral in Fagatele Bay. It is unclear what has caused this damage. It could result from bomb-fishing, anchors, storm waves tossing loose dead coral plates (background), or even foraging by turtles, all of which are known to occur. *Photo: E. Lyman*

national marine sanctuary, but this disaster helped to propel the decision for the site's designation.

The soft tissues of coral are consumed when crown-of-thorns starfish feeds, leaving behind the hard coral skeleton. As long as other aspects of the ecosystem are intact and new disturbances do not occur, new coral recruitment and growth will replace the damage caused by the starfish. The reefs of American Samoa are resilient because coralline algae rapidly colonizes the dead coral skeletons and cements reef surfaces together to promote the settlement and growth of new coral colonies. Without this rapid colonization by coralline algae, wave action can cause the dead coral skeletons to fragment and turn to rubble before the new coral community can establish.

Tropical Cyclones

American Samoa is susceptible to tropical cyclones during the southern summer from November to April. In 1990, 1991, 2004 and 2005, cyclones caused decreases in coral coverage and abundance in American Samoa and damaged the reef framework to varying degrees. When severe, damage produced large amounts of coral rubble and redistributed sediments in shallow water. On Feb. 4, 1990, Tropical Cyclone Ofa passed about 225 kilometers to the southwest of Tutuila Island. Although the wind speed associated with this storm was not exceptionally strong during its passage, storm waves and storm surge generated by the

A plague of crown-of-thorns starfish ravaged the reefs of Fagatele Bay in the late 1970s. *Photo: C. Birkeland*

Reef survey after Hurricane Val in 1992. The survey was taken to assess the damage that the hurricane caused to the reef. *Photo: Harold Hudson*

Bleached coral in American Samoa in 1994. *Photo: Peter Craig*

cyclone caused damage to Fagatele Bay reefs. On Dec. 10, 1991, Tropical Cyclone Val caused severe damage to the fringing reef systems and coastal areas of Tutuila. Together, Ofa and Val inflicted considerable damage to the reef communities within the bay. While the impacts of Heta in 2004 and Olaf in 2005 were less severe on Fagatele Bay, they caused significant damage in other parts of the archipelago.

One of the most conspicuous effects of cyclones is the stripping away of many of dead and living corals, thus producing a large amount of new rubble and shingle, which undergoes considerable redistribution on the order of tens to hundreds of meters. Some structural damage occurs to the reef as well, particularly at the reef margin and reef slope zones, where sections of reef buttresses, pinnacles, and knobs can topple. However, as stated above, the coral populations of American Samoa have proven to be resilient to these damaging events and coral populations currently are in a phase of rapid recovery.

Elevated Ocean Temperature

In the summers of 1994, 2002 and 2003, Fagatele Bay experienced one of its most significant natural threats—unusually warm water surrounded American Samoa for several months and caused corals to "bleach," or to lose their pigment-carrying symbiotic algae partners (zooxanthellae). These algae normally live within the tissues of the coral animal and give the coral its color. A bleached coral appears brilliantly white due to the transparency of coral tissue without its zooxanthellae. Though bleaching is not always lethal, many corals were killed as a result of these bleaching events.

These recent bleaching events have been caused by increases in sea-surface temperatures as a result of regional El Niño

events and possibly the result of global warming. Only a slight increase above normal water temperature is required to initiate bleaching. It can be caused by a short-term exposure (1-2 days) to temperature elevations of 3 to 4 °C, or by long-term exposure (weeks) to elevations of only 1 to 2 °C. Corals can recover from bleaching if temperatures return to normal and the coral regains its symbiotic algae. However, if temperature conditions remain anomalously high for an extended period, or bleaching is particularly severe, bleached coral will die. Bleaching has been observed nearly every summer over the last decade. It affects corals mostly in shallow water, but has been observed as deep as 40 meters (130 feet).

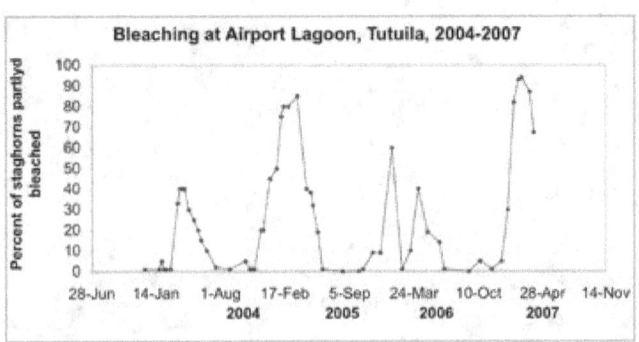

Bleaching of staghorn coral in the airport lagoon on Tutuila, American Samoa.. *Source: Doug Fenner, territorial Coral Reef Monitoring Program.*

Fishing

Although most fishing methods are prohibited in Fagatele Bay National Marine Sanctuary, the sanctuary's remote location makes enforcement of regulations difficult. There is significant evidence that the bay is, in fact, being fished. Several large species of reef fish that are characteristic of unfished reefs in the Indo-Pacific region are conspicuously absent or are small in size in Fagatele Bay. These include species such as Maori wrasse (humphead wrasse; Napoleon wrasse; *Cheilinus undulates*), sharks, and large species of grouper and parrotfish, all of which are known to be particularly vulnerable to fishing pressure. Given that many of these species are more abundant and larger in size elsewhere in the Pacific where fishing is banned, these observations suggest that fishing pressure on the reefs of American Samoa and Fagatele Bay has had a significant impact on fish populations.

Because of its remote location and limited access from land, direct observation of fishing activity, both legal and illegal, is difficult to obtain; however, it is likely that poachers fish in the sanctuary when weather conditions permit. Most recently, in December 2005 law enforcement officials apprehended illegal fishermen in the sanctuary. Fishermen have the potential to very quickly reduce the population of commercial reef fish species in a small area such as Fagatele Bay. One particularly efficient harvesting technique is spearfishing at night using SCUBA equipment. Many targeted species rest on the reef during the night, making them easy targets for night fishermen. The Government of American Samoa banned SCUBA spearfishing in 2001 because of concerns by local scientists about declines in fish numbers once this technique became widely used.

Evidence also suggests that fishing with explosives — an unsustainable form of fishing that is inexpensive, quick, and efficient, as well as highly destructive — has occurred in the bay. A 2001 survey found a large *Porites* sp. coral colony that was severely damaged. The colony had recently been split in two, and

Porites coral head in Fagatele Bay showing a large fracture created by explosives used to harvest fish. *Photo: C. Birkeland*

one side appeared to have been reduced to rubble. It is likely that explosives caused this damage, because approximately 9 meters of detonation cord was found adjacent to the coral colony. This colony is exceptionally large, and given the slow growth rate of this species, is estimated to be approximately 800 years of age. Although the damage can still be seen, the colony remains healthy away from the fracture. In June 2005, a new spate of fishing with explosives was documented in Fagatele Bay. A reward for information yielded no suspects, but did bring attention to the problem and a public desire for the apprehension of anyone fishing in this manner.

Diseases

Outbreaks of disease on coral reefs can cause significant changes in community structure, species diversity and abundance of reef organisms. Diseases of coralline algae and corals have been documented in Fagatele Bay. These afflictions are monitored in order to be on guard for increases in their occurrence. Coralline lethal orange disease is a bacterial infection that affects encrusting coralline algae. It is identified by its bright orange color and the white dead areas it produces on affected algae. A 2004 study found that, of seven sites examined around Tutuila, coralline lethal orange disease was most prevalent in Fagatele Bay. Another disease of coralline algae is a black fungal infection that has only been reported in American Samoa.

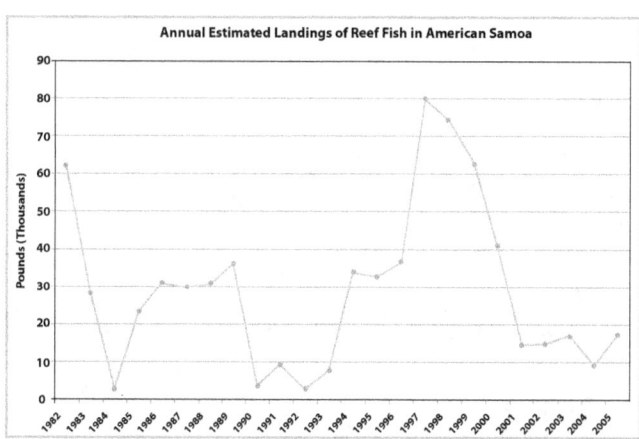

Estimated weight of coral reef fish caught in American Samoa from 1982 to 2005. The period of high landings from 1997 to 2000 was during a time of intense spearfishing using SCUBA in the territory. This practice was banned in 2001, but its impact may still be evident in the low numbers of large parrotfish and large predatory fish (the usual target of such fishing) on American Samoa's reefs, including those in Fagatele Bay, in 2006. *Source: Dept. of Marine and Wildlife Resources*

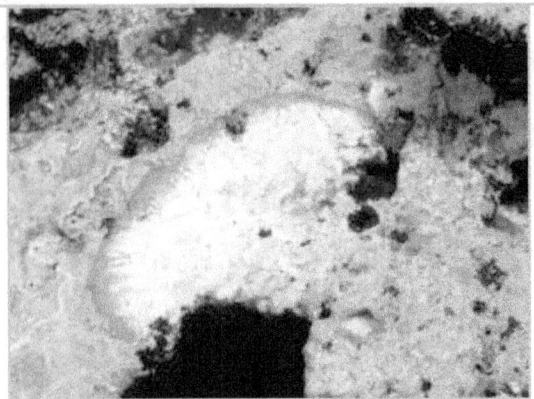

Coralline lethal orange disease in Fagatele Bay National Marine Sanctuary.
Photo: Bill Kiene

One of the most common coral diseases found in the waters of Tutuila is white syndrome. Due to the difficulty of differentiating between the coral diseases that are white in appearance, both white band and white plague diseases are placed in a category known as "white syndrome." A symptom of white syndrome disease is a distinct line or band of bleached infected coral tissue, between exposed coral skeleton and healthy coral tissue. This disease can be virulent and results in the rapid death of coral tissue. Another condition that may be a disease and is often observed around Tutuila involves skeletal growth anomalies (hyperplasms), which cause distorted, tumor-like growths on the surface of the coral.

Agriculture

Agriculture in American Samoa is still largely a subsistence sector with mostly traditional staple food crops, chickens and pigs. The 1999 Agriculture Census of American Samoa reported that about 41 percent of the territorial land area is being farmed, and nearly 6,500 farms were reported with an average farm size of about three acres. Of these, about 1,100 were classified as commercial operations. A farm was defined as any place that raised or produced any agricultural products for sale or consumption. Approximately 75 percent of households in American Samoa fit this description.

With an increasing population and a fragile economy, American Samoa is likely to experience an increase in agricultural development, including the land surrounding Fagatele Bay. Such development may threaten water quality, habitat integrity and biological health of Fagatele Bay if soil and sediment runoff into the bay is not controlled. With two-thirds of American Samoa's 197 square kilometers having slopes greater than 30 percent and a rainfall of up to 5,000 millimeters per year, soil erosion is a constant threat. Clearing of land for agriculture within watersheds often decreases the ability of soils to absorb rainfall. Without proper land management, streams carry eroded soils, fertilizers and pesticides into nearshore waters. The developed watersheds around Tutuila generally discharge higher sediment loads than undeveloped areas. The steep topography of Fagatele Bay's watershed is particularly vulnerable to erosion once the land is cleared.

Taro, a perennial plant with an edible tuber, is one of the most important staple crops in American Samoa. It is inherently part of the traditions, customs and culture of the Samoans, and adherence to traditional cultivation practices can help reduce environmental impacts. These traditional practices include leaving trees to reduce erosion, cutting weeds to use as mulch, and using a planting stick (the oso) rather than tilling the soil. Unfortunately, these practices are often replaced by the removal

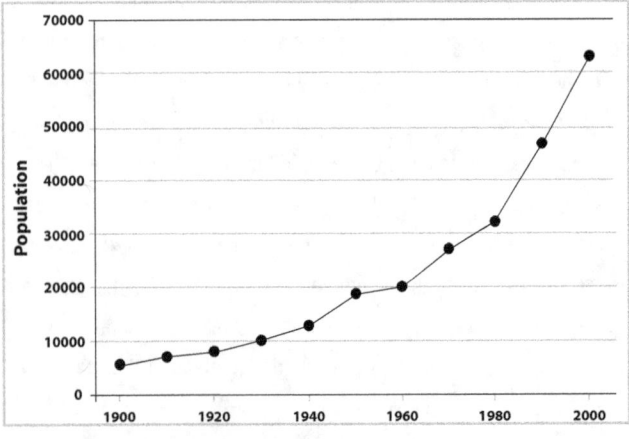

Population growth in American Samoa. *Source: U.S. Census Bureau.*

Taro is the most important staple crop in American Samoa. If careful cultivation methods are not used on steep slopes, substantial soil erosion will occur.
Photo: Larry S. Hirata, A.S. Community College

Land cleared for agriculture on the ridge-slope above Fagatele Bay in 2006.
Photo: Bill Kiene

of all vegetation and leaving fields to sit fallow after cultivation. Once the land is cleared, it will take decades for the forest to recover to its natural state. Without careful stewardship, forest re-growth in cleared areas may be inhibited by the rapid invasion of vines and other plant species. These invasive plants replace the native trees and ground cover with vegetation that cannot efficiently hold soil in place. This choking of the native forest by vines and other invasive species can be seen in parts of Fagatele Bay's watershed. Over the last year, landowners have cleared new areas of the slopes above Fagatele Bay for taro cultivation. This creates significant concern for the integrity of the forest ecosystem, its soil, and the bay's water quality.

Visitation

There is relatively little tourism in American Samoa and it is likely to be some years before the territory enters the mainstream of South Pacific tourism. The annual number of visitors to the National Park of American Samoa is currently estimated to be only 1,000 on Tutuila Island, 1,000 on Ofu Island, and 20 on Ta'u Island. About half of these tourists use marine areas of the park for swimming, snorkeling, or scuba diving. There are also few pleasure boats — about 30 anchor in Pago Pago Harbor during the cyclone season, but none are found elsewhere in the territory. Tournaments for pelagic sport fish (e.g., tuna, marlin, etc.) occur sporadically, with some 20 small local vessels competing to catch the largest fish (Peter et al. 2005). Visiting Fagatele Bay sanctuary is difficult even in good weather due to its remote location and the nature of the terrain that surrounds the bay. Because the land is privately owned, permission is also needed from the landowners to access the bay by land. Little is known about the number of people who

visit the bay on a daily basis, but official patrols and visits by sanctuary staff over the past 18 years indicate those numbers are very low.

There are few locally owned pleasure boats. Yachts come to Pago Pago Harbor to buy provisions and find shelter during the cyclone season. Sportfishing for pelagic tuna, mahi mahi and marlin is popular and occasional fishing tournaments are held, but these activities occur in offshore waters rather than on the coastal reefs. There are no commercial SCUBA diving operators presently in the territory, but the potential to attract sport divers to Fagatele Bay and the territory's coral reefs exists.

Despite the low numbers of visitors, human impacts on coral reefs surrounding Tutuila Island, including Fagatele Bay, have the potential to be severe. Documented impacts due to visitation of the bay are unregulated fishing, illegal collection of corals and other invertebrates, and damage to the reef from boat anchors and walking on the reef flat. Anchor damage has been observed, and in response, two mooring buoys were installed in 2006 to allow boaters to visit the bay without dropping anchor. Discarded trash is also a potential problem caused by both land and sea visitors to the bay.

Rapidly growing vines are inhibiting growth of the natural forest in parts of Fagatele Bay's watershed. This is the consequence of abandoning cleared land after using it for cultivation. The vines have also invaded virgin forest adjacent to the formally cultivated area. Photo: Bill Kiene

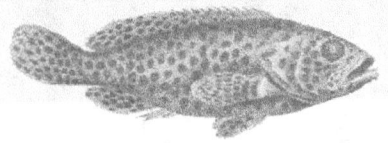

State of Sanctuary Resources

Overview

This section provides summaries of the condition and trends within four resource areas: water, habitat, living resources and archaeological resources. For each, sanctuary staff and selected outside experts considered a series of questions about each resource area. Answers are supported by specific examples of data, investigations, monitoring and observations, and the basis for judgment is provided in the text and summarized in the table for each resource area. Where published or additional information exists, the reader is provided with appropriate references and Web links.

Water

American Samoa has nearly 240 kilometers of coastline. Fringing coral reefs characterize the coastal embayments and open coastal waters. Pollution from poorly constructed human and pig waste disposal systems, increased turbidity and nutrients from soil erosion, pose the greatest threats to near-shore water quality in American Samoa. Solid waste from improper trash disposal adds another significant threat to coastal waters.

With over a century of development, Pago Pago Harbor is the most populated and industrialized embayment in American Samoa. In addition to the non-point source pollution mentioned above, Pago Pago Harbor is potentially affected by pollution from marina and port traffic and a small shipyard. In the outer harbor, regulated effluent from the tuna canneries and sewage treatment plant is discharged. Due to the segregation and transportation of cannery waste beyond the inner harbor, better treatment of sewage, and more effective monitoring and prosecution of commercial vessels that pollute the harbor, the water quality in the inner harbor has greatly improved in the last decade.

Outside the harbor, offshore waters of American Samoa are low in nutrients and other contaminants in part because they are rapidly diluted to open ocean conditions. High-strength wastes (solids, nitrogen, phosphorus) from the tuna canneries are dumped in a designated offshore area approximately eight kilometers south of Tutuila. From data collected by the canneries,

Hidey holes fish. *Photo: FBNMS*

Humpback whales often breed and calve in Samoan waters. *Photo: Paul Brown*

the waste is considered to have only a localized effect on the marine environment. As a result, Fagatele Bay is considered to be unaffected by any pollution that leaves the harbor or by the cannery waste.

The municipal landfill for Tutuila is less than one and a half kilometers from Fagatele Bay. Although separated from Fagatele Bay by the high ridge that surrounds the bay, this landfill has the potential to leach contaminants into groundwater that flows into Fagatele Bay. Monitoring of groundwater and springs in the vicinity is needed to be sure this facility is not affecting water quality.

A direct threat to Fagatele Bay is the increase in water temperature that can cause corals to bleach. This phenomenon has occurred more often in recent years throughout the territory.

Summary Assessment of Water Conditions

The following is an assessment by sanctuary staff and American Samoa marine researchers of water quality in Fagatele Bay National Marine Sanctuary and how it may be affecting the environment:

Are specific or multiple stressors, including changing oceanographic and atmospheric conditions, affecting water quality and how are they changing?

High water clarity and the bay's rich biodiversity and apparent resilience would suggest that water quality in Fagatele Bay is good. However, the frequency with which high sea temperatures are causing corals to bleach and die is increasing. For this reason, water quality based on stressors is considered to be only fair. Temperature impacts on bleaching are expected by many to intensify in the future.

What is the eutrophic condition of sanctuary waters and how is it changing?

Nutrient levels in the bay are currently low, as is appropriate for a tropical coral reef. However, there is concern that land clearing and associated human habitation in Fagatele Bay's watershed may be increasing nutrient levels near streams and beaches used by residents. At present, this activity is not considered to be changing nutrient conditions offshore, but measures are needed to ensure this does not reduce the bay's water quality in the future.

Do sanctuary waters pose risks to human health and how are they changing?

Sanctuary waters do not appear to pose risks to human health. However, an assessment of the potential effects of the nearby landfill on ground and marine waters is needed.

What are the levels of human activities that may influence water quality and how are they changing?

Extensive land clearing for agriculture on the east side of the bay has impacted the forest and may have compromised its ability to prevent soil and sediments from entering sanctuary waters.

Water Quality Status & Trends

Good	Good/Fair	Fair	Fair/Poor	Poor	Undet.

▲ = Improving ▬ = Not changing ▼ = Getting Worse
? = Undetermined trend N/A = Question not applicable

Status	Trend	Basis for Judgment
Stressors	▼	Increasing number of warm-water events causing coral bleaching
Eutrophic Condition	▬	Low nutrient levels, good water clarity; lack of fleshy algae
Human Health	?	No known risks
Human Activities	▼	Land clearing for agriculture, proximity of island landfill

Habitat

A series of reef surveys starting in the early 1980s for Tutuila and Fagatele Bay suggests that in the early to mid-1980s, hard coral cover was increasing. An outbreak of crown-of-thorns starfish in 1978 had killed 90 percent of the corals in the bay, and the increases seen in the 1980s demonstrate the recovery from that event. Then, in 1990 and 1991 coral populations were reduced by severe tropical cyclones. A mass-bleaching event in 1994 killed many of the remaining corals. Since that time, survey results show coral populations have recovered. According to the most recent surveys (2005), coral covers an average of 40 percent of reef surfaces. Crustose coralline algae dominates the remainder of reef surfaces, which, together with high levels of grazing by fish, encourages new coral recruitment and growth. These cycles of coral destruction and subsequent recovery and re-growth attest to the resilience of the reef ecosystem in Fagatele Bay.

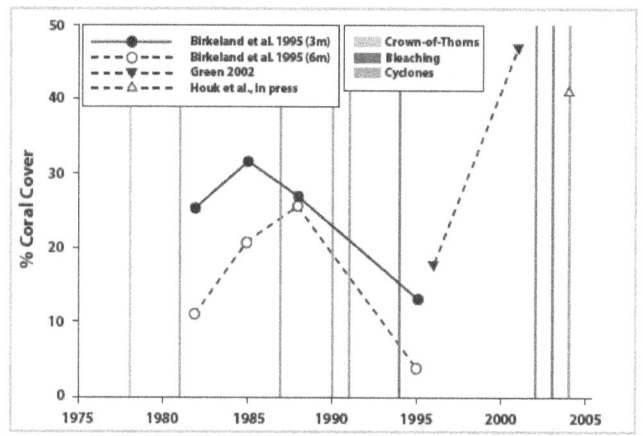

Hard coral cover trends for Tutuila from three studies show periods of recovery interrupted by events causing mortality. *Sources: Birkeland et al. 1997, Green 2002, Houk et al. 2005.*

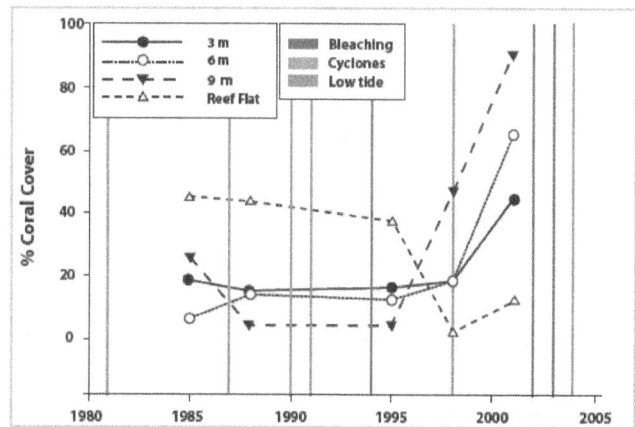

Hard coral cover trends for Fagatele Bay (Birkeland et al. 2004). Surveys on the reef slope in 2004 and 2005, while not directly comparable to these data, indicated there has been no decline, and probably an increase, in coral cover. *Sources: Green et al. 2005, Whaylen and Fenner 2005*

New coral colonies grow on the grey-pink, coralline algae encrusted surface of a large dead table coral. *Photo: Richard Murphy, Ocean Futures Society*

New life from old: coralline algae and juvenile coral colonies re-build the reef after the death of a coral. *Photo: Richard Murphy, Ocean Futures Society*

Surveys at different depths show that different habitats have experienced different patterns of coral cover through time. From 1985 through 2001, reef slope surveys found coral cover to be low, increasing to high levels in 2002. Surveys of coral on the reef flat found the opposite pattern, with the highest cover from 1985 to 1995 and low levels in 1997 and 2002.

The reef flat and reef slope are very different habitats due to exposure to wave action, low tide events and extremes in water temperature. Coral cover did not increase from 1985 to 1995 as a result of the three cyclones and the major bleaching event that damaged coral populations during this period. The loss of live hard corals on the reef flat after 1995 was due to a series of extreme low-tide events in 1998. Coral cover had increased in all habitats by 2001 and surveys in 2004 and 2005 indicate this trend continues.

Summary Assessment of Habitat Conditions

The following information provides an assessment by sanctuary staff and American Samoa marine researchers of the status and trends pertaining to marine habitat:

What are the abundance and distribution of major habitat types and how are they changing?

Corals are the primary builder of habitats in Fagatele Bay and their abundance and distribution control, to a large extent, the numbers of other invertebrates and fishes.

Coral populations in Fagatele Bay are presently diverse (200 species) and abundant, and they have increased following a series of destructive events in the 1980s and 1990s. However, the trend in coral cover is uncertain because the apparent natural resilience of the system may be affected by an increase in potentially destructive fishing activities in the bay and the potential for increasing periods of coral bleaching due to high water temperature.

What is the condition of biologically structured habitats and how is it changing?

As a result of coral recovery from several destructive events, and in spite of some coral diseases, the condition of the biologically structured habitats is generally good and does not appear to be changing.

What are the contaminant concentrations in sanctuary habitats and how are they changing?

Contaminants do not appear to be present in the reef structure or in the sediments.

What are the levels of human activities that may influence habitat quality and how are they changing?

Although some human-induced damage has occurred, the level of human activity is relatively low and does not appear to be changing.

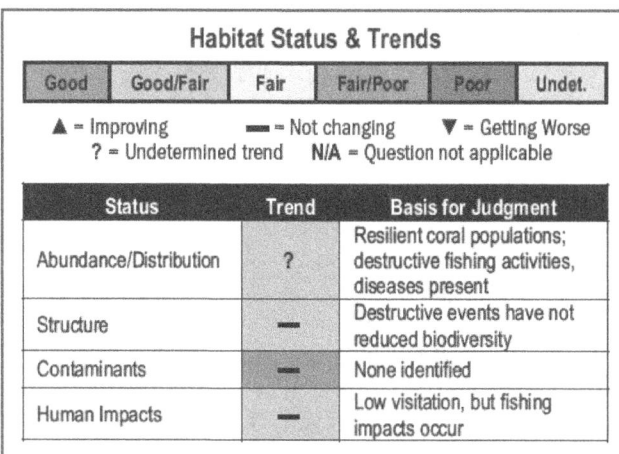

Habitat Status & Trends

Good	Good/Fair	Fair	Fair/Poor	Poor	Undet.

▲ = Improving   ━ = Not changing   ▼ = Getting Worse
? = Undetermined trend   N/A = Question not applicable

Status	Trend	Basis for Judgment
Abundance/Distribution	?	Resilient coral populations; destructive fishing activities, diseases present
Structure	━	Destructive events have not reduced biodiversity
Contaminants	━	None identified
Human Impacts	━	Low visitation, but fishing impacts occur

Living Resources

Corals and Coralline Algae

The abundance of corals and coralline algae in Fagatele Bay, as discussed above, indicates considerable ecosystem resilience. Natural events such as cyclones, crown-of-thorns population explosions and low-tide events have resulted in extreme but relatively short-lived interruptions in coral growth. Coral cover fluctuations, especially in shallow water, have approached 40 percent over very short (decadal) intervals owing to high levels of recruitment and growth, which are likely stimulated by good water quality and high coralline algae cover.

Scientsts and managers are concerned, however, that r cently identified threats could undermine continued resilience of Fagatele Bay's coral reefs. These include increasing levels and frequency of coral bleaching (perhaps resulting from increasing water temperature), increasing occurrence of diseases that affect corals and coralline algae, and the impacts of certain destructive fishing techniques. Together, these additional threats could diminish important characteristics of the reef Coralline lethal orange disease could significantly reduce coralline algae abundance, which could result in coral recruitment reduction. Also of concern is that diseases among corals could spread quickly in the dense populations that currently exist in Fagatele Bay. Blast fishing destabilizes reef surfaces and puts corals at additional risk during high energy events such as storms. Given these threats, it is expected that the recovery capacity of reef populations will be less than previous observations suggested

following future natural disturbances.

Fish

There is currently debate as to why populations of large carnivorous fishes are low on the coral reefs in American Samoa. The narrow fringing reefs that drop quickly into deep water may limit the extent of critical shallow water habitats as well as the extent of off-reef forage areas for these fishes. However, most of the reef fish species expected to be found in American Samoa are seen and periodically caught by fishermen. Their small size and numbers suggest fishing is keeping these fishes from recovering to levels that would be expected on reefs in the region.

Reef fish are harvested in both subsistence and artisanal fisheries on the five main islands of the territory. Artisanal fishing includes both nighttime free-divers who spear reef fish and small boat fishers who target deepwater bottomfish. There is currently no export of coral reef fish to off-island markets or the aquarium trade.

Subsistence fishing has declined steadily over the past two decades as American Samoa has shifted from a subsistence to a cash-based economy, suggesting the size and number of targeted species should be increasing. Even so, while small surgeonfish

A fisherman on Tutuila with a large Maori wrasse. These fish have become extremely rare on American Samoa's reefs. *Photo: Leslie Whalen*

and parrotfish are abundant, the number and size of other larger coral reef fishes such as grouper and snapper are small. It is unclear if the present fishing effort or other factors continue to suppress recovery of these fish populations. Furthermore, the ecological impacts of changing size structure in the fish community would include not only changes in the abundance of non-targeted species, but cascading effects that involve reductions in herbivory and perhaps increases in leafy algae abundance that alter benthic community structure. It will be important to include these parameters within the monitoring program to both understand them better and respond appropriately to changes. Also, carefully controlled experiments are necessary to determine the effects of present fishing pressures.

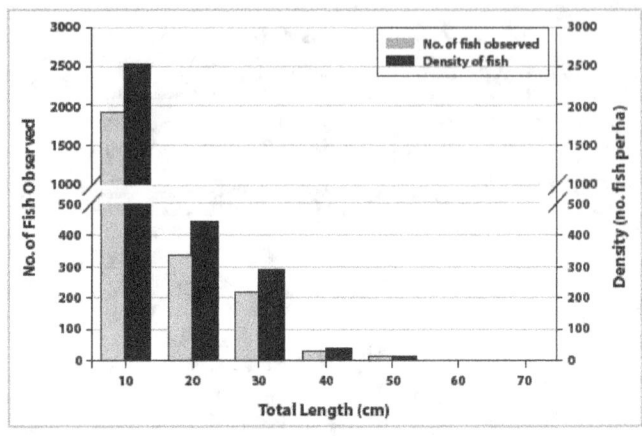

Size of targeted fishes at 17 sites on Tutuila in 2002. Source: Green 2002

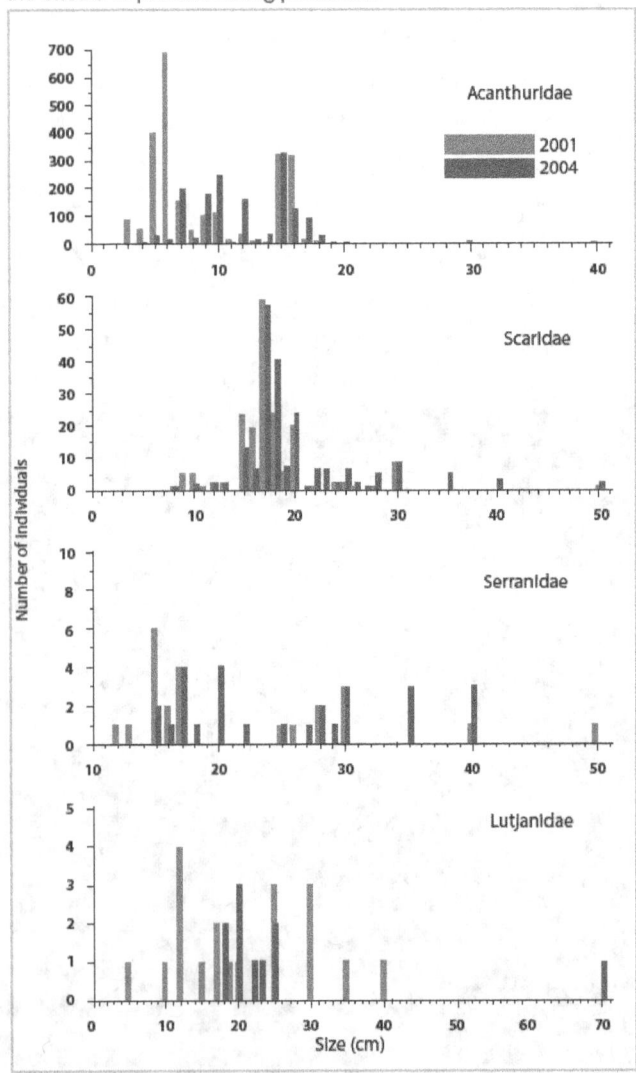

Size structure of populations of important fisheries species in Fagatele Bay.
Source: Green, Miller and Mundy 2005

There are two types of monitoring programs in the territory that document characteristics of fish populations. First, underwater visual surveys (fisheries-independent surveys) describe the types of fish observed by divers on the reef. Second, surveys of fish harvests or creel surveys (fisheries-dependent surveys) document the actual species and quantities of fish extracted from the reefs. The Department of Marine and Wildlife Resources has monitored artisanal catches since 1982, but harvests by night-divers and subsistence fisheries have been monitored only intermittently.

Territory-wide visual fish surveys document that large fish are rare on the reefs around the five main islands, a strong indication that populations have been overfished. These include sharks, Maori wrasse, and large species of grouper and parrotfish. The surveys indicate that reefs have had few large fish for at least eight years. Additionally, the surveys show that densities of large fish are higher on American Samoa's remote reefs (Swains Island and Rose Atoll).

It is critically important to understand the direct relationship between fishing pressure and the character of fish populations in American Samoa. This understanding will likely not be gained until functioning no-take areas are established and monitored. Fagatele Bay National Marine Sanctuary regulations still allow fishing, but put restrictions on how fish are caught. Through its upcoming management plan review process, the sanctuary could become a no-take area and provide a valuable laboratory for understanding the role of fishing in structuring fish populations in American Samoa.

A hawksbill turtle in American Samoa. The adult hawksbill can reach a meter (3 feet) long and weigh over 90 kilograms (200 pounds) and is caught for food and its beautiful carapace, or shell, which is used to manufacture jewelry and other products. *Photo: Emma Hickerson*

Sea Turtles

Turtles play an important role in Samoan culture. In one village adjacent to Fagatele Bay, villagers "call" a turtle and shark, which are said to come to shore when the villagers sing a special song. The song recounts a legend of the village sheltering two Western Samoan visitors, who in gratitude vowed to return as a turtle and shark whenever their hosts sang their story to the sea. Turtles are also believed to save fishermen who are lost at sea. For these reasons, the Samoan word for sea turtle is "I'asa," which translates as "sacred fish."

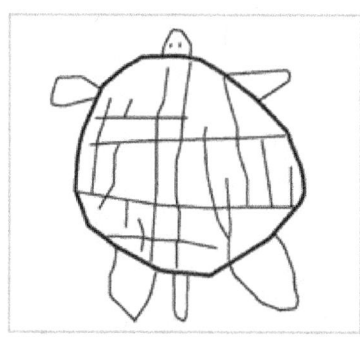

Trace of a turtle petroglyph on coastal rocks near Fagatele Bay sanctuary. *Source: Craig 2005*

Samoans traditionally harvested sea turtles for food. Turtle shells were made into jewelry, ceremonial decorations and utilitarian items. Federal and territorial laws now protect turtles and their eggs from harvest in American Samoa's waters and on its beaches.

Hawksbill and green turtles are the most common species in the area, and hawksbills nest on beaches of Tutuila. There is one report of a turtle nesting on one of the small beaches of Fagatele Bay.

Sea turtle populations have declined, both locally and throughout the South Pacific, due to harvest, loss of nesting beach habitats and incidental catches in fishing gear. In American Samoa, a few turtles and their eggs are still illegally harvested, but public education programs have helped to make people aware that turtle populations are seriously threatened, some with extinction, if such harvests continue. In 2003, American Samoa established a sanctuary for sea turtles and marine mammals in its territorial waters (0-3 miles offshore).

Marine Mammals

Southern humpback whales migrate from their Antarctic feeding grounds to American Samoa to calve and mate between July and October. Some individuals documented in American Samoa waters have also been recorded in other parts of the South Pacific, but their migratory patterns within the region are unclear. Other marine mammals, such as sperm whales, rough-toothed and spinner dolphins, and false killer whales occur in American Samoa's waters. NOAA initiated annual marine mammal surveys around Tutuila in 2003. Photographs are taken of flukes and DNA analysis of tissue samples allows comparisons with populations in other regions. Whale populations in American Samoa show low incidence of fishing gear entanglements.

Summary Assessment of Living Resources Conditions

The following information provides an assessment by sanctuary staff and American Samoa marine researchers of the status and trends pertaining to the sanctuary's living resources:

What is the status of biodiversity and how is it changing?

Biodiversity in the Fagatele Bay sanctuary does not appear to be changing. Fish diversity in Fagatele Bay is higher than most other sites on Tutuila. However, individual numbers of some fish species are lower than expected.

What is the status of environmentally sustainable fishing and how is it changing?

In spite of restrictions on fishing, the difficulties of enforcement allow illegal fishing in Fagatele Bay to occur; this appears to have caused declines in some grouper, wrasse, and snapper populations. At present, fish populations are dominated by surgeonfish and parrotfish. While continued fishing may cause further declines, populations currently do not appear to be changing.

What is the status of non-indigenous species and how is it changing?

Taxonomic studies of marine species present in American Samoa (including Fagatele Bay) have found non-indigenous and cryptogenic (of uncertain origin) invertebrate and algae species, but these mainly occur in Pago Pago Harbor and are not considered to significantly impact Fagatele Bay sanctuary. Certain invertebrates, such as zoanthids, have been known to rapidly colonize disturbed reef surfaces, slowing the recovery of coral populations.

What is the status of key species and how is it changing?

Fishing has reduced the size and number of predatory fish species, particularly grouper and snapper, to the extent that large individuals are rarely seen; at present, their population levels do not appear to be changing.

What is the condition or health of key species and how is it changing?

Disease has increasingly afflicted some corals and coralline algae and there is concern that these additional stressors could reduce the reef's ability to recover from natural disturbances. In addition, abundant herbivorous fishes keep fleshy algae populations low.

What are the levels of human activities that may influence living resource quality and how are they changing?

Illegal and legal fishing, including primarily subsistence and artisanal fishing, continues to remove large fish. Even though subsistence fishing appears to be developing, population recovery has not been observed. It is unclear what other factors, including illegal fishing, may be hampering recovery.

Humpback whale. Photo: HIHWNMS

Living Resources Status & Trends

Good	Good/Fair	Fair	Fair/Poor	Poor	Undet.

▲ = Improving — = Not changing ▼ = Getting Worse
? = Undetermined trend N/A = Question not applicable

Status	Trend	Basis for Judgment
Biodiversity	—	A l species present but some in low numbers
Extracted Species	—	Fishing has removed large fish
Invasive Species	—	Some non-indigenous algae and invertebrates may be present
Key Species	—	Reduced numbers and size of certain predatory fish species
Health of Key Species	▼	Coral and coralline algae diseases
Human Activities	?	Illegal a d legal fishing cont nues to remove large fish

Maritime Archaeological Resources

No marine archaeological artifacts have been found in Fagatele Bay National Marine Sanctuary.

Maritime Archaeological Resources Status & Trends

Good	Good/Fair	Fair	Fair/Poor	Poor	Undet.

▲ = Improving — = Not changing ▼ = Getting Worse
? = Undetermined trend N/A = Question not applicable

Status	Trend	Basis for Judgment
Integrity	N/A	No documented underwater archeological sites
Threat to Environment	N/A	No documented underwater archeological sites
Human Activities	N/A	No documented underwater archeological sites

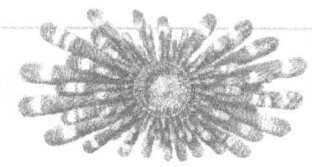

Response to Pressures

Overview

The Fagatele Bay sanctuary staff works closely with its American Samoa government partners to promote sound use, conservation and awareness of the sanctuary's marine environment. The sanctuary staff also works throughout the territory to help the people of American Samoa understand and better utilize its marine resources.

The American Samoa government coordinates all of its territorial coral reef management activities through the Coral Reef Advisory Group. This group comprises both territorial and federal agencies, including the American Samoa Department of Commerce (which includes the American Samoa Coastal Management Program and Fagatele Bay sanctuary), the Department of Marine and Wildlife Resources, the American Samoa Environmental Protection Agency, the American Samoa Community College, and the National Park of American Samoa. These agencies collaborate to plan and implement actions related to the management of the territory's coral reefs.

Each agency within the Coral Reef Advisory Group has specific projects and programs that enhance the quality of marine habitats, regulate activities on coral reefs, promote awareness, and facilitate research into various aspects of coral reef science. The Coral Reef Advisory Group helps to coordinate these efforts and build collaborative projects, using a threat-based approach to identify key problems on American Samoa's reefs. In tandem with this, the advisory group has also created four three-year action strategies to address the issues of overfishing, global climate change, land-based sources of pollution, and population pressure (the first three were identified in this report as significant concerns for Fagatele Bay sanctuary). The U.S. Coral Reef Initiative has been instrumental in supporting the territory in its coral reef conservation activities. The Coral Conservation Grant Program has provided managers and scientists in American Samoa with staff, funds, and equipment with which to accomplish key research and management projects.

The sanctuary staff works with the Coral Reef Advisory Group's education and outreach coordinator to increase public awareness of issues affecting American Samoa's coral reefs. In addition to

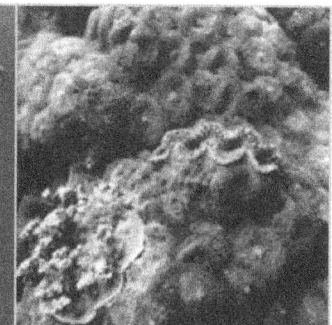

Spinner dolphin. *Photo: Ed Lyman*   Giant clam. *Photo: Ed Lyman*

regular school visits, current projects include education grants to teachers for the materials and supplies necessary for coral reef lessons and projects, development of marine education brochures and production of a monthly newspaper article, published in both English and Samoan.

Water

With its low human impact, Fagatele Bay provides a baseline for other sampling sites around Tutuila; therefore, partner organizations have begun collaborating in monitoring the water quality in the Fagatele Bay sanctuary. Water samples collected by the American Samoa Community College and analyzed by the American Samoa Environmental Protection Agency are used to measure *Enterococcus* bacterial concentrations. This collaboration is important in assessing how development of land, such as forest clearing and agricultural development, around Fagatele Bay may affect its water quality in the future. American Samoa water quality standards and sanctuary regulations aim to prevent any reduction in water quality in Fagatele Bay.

Fagatele Bay sanctuary staff is also working with the NOAA Pacific Islands Fisheries Service Center to monitor water temperature. Near real-time water temperature is now available on the web through the Coral Reef Ecosystem Division of the National Marine Fisheries Service, Pacific Islands Fisheries Center (http://crei.pifsc.noaa.gov/ocean_data.html).

With the assistance of U. S. Geological Survey scientists, a proposal is being prepared to assess the groundwater beneath the island landfill to determine if contaminants are leaching into the aquifer and being transported to the marine environment. The landfill is on the other side of the ridge, immediately north of the sanctuary. Geologists believe groundwater beneath the landfill may flow south toward Fagatele Bay and Larsen Bay, and may discharge in coastal or submarine springs.

Habitat

National Marine Sanctuary Program regulations prohibit activities that disturb or damage the natural features of Fagatele Bay sanctuary. This includes destructive fishing methods and anchoring. With the help of a recent NOAA research cruise to American Samoa, two mooring buoys were installed in the sanctuary in 2006 to eliminate the need for boats to anchor. Submerged logs were also removed from the reef to stop their movement and prevent damage to corals.

Living Resources

Fagatele Bay is divided into two subzones that regulate where certain fishing activities can occur within the sanctuary. Zone A includes the area from the high water mark of the inner bay to a line between Fagatele Point and Matautuloa Point. Zone B covers the area between the boundary of zone A and a line between Fagatele Point and Steps Point. Present sanctuary regulations prohibit removing or disturbing any marine invertebrate or plant in either zone. Most fishing gears are excluded from the sanctuary. The fishing gear that can be used in zone B are fishing poles and hand lines, both of which are prohibited in zone A. The use of other fishing gears, including nets and spears, is prohibited in both zones. All sea turtles are protected, and ensnaring or trapping them is prohibited in the sanctuary, as well as anywhere in American Samoa waters.

The sanctuary protects marine mammals and birds from "take," disturbance and harm. These animals are also protected in territorial and federal waters under the U.S. Marine Mammal Protection Act, the Endangered Species Act and the Migratory Bird Treaty Act.

The sanctuary staff coordinates scientific research and monitoring of the ecological conditions in the bay. The program has built collaborations with local scientists of the Department of Marine and Wildlife Resources, as well as U.S. university-based

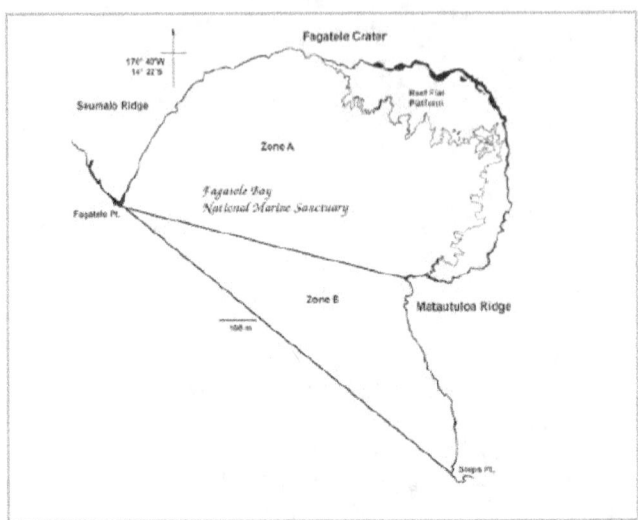

Map of Fagatele Bay sanctuary showing zones A and B, which regulate fishing activities. The use of fishing gear is prohibited in zone A and only line fishing is allowed in zone B.

scientists, to conduct regular field assessments of coral and fish populations, coral diseases and other indicators of coral reef health in Fagatele Bay. The data collected adds to one of the largest coral reef monitoring datasets in the world, helping to gauge the long-term patterns of change and recovery from events that have disrupted the ecosystem in the past and may cause disruptions in the future. A summary of data collected over 25 years of monitoring in Fagatele Bay will be published in a book chapter by Dr. Charles Birkeland in 2008. The sanctuary looks forward to using this information to make informed management decisions, evaluate the effectiveness of the monitoring program itself, and update the sanctuary's management plan.

Fagatele Bay also has a substantial geographic information system (GIS) data archive, developed in partnership with the America Samoa Department of Commerce, NOAA and researchers at Oregon State University and University of South Florida. GIS data are available from shallow-water multi-beam bathymetric surveys, submersible dives, and ecological surveys conducted from 2001-2006. NOAA's Coral Reef Ecosystem Division collected substantial mapping and ecological data on three research cruises to American Samoa and is compiling much of the information for Fagatele Bay into a report and database. Near real-time sea surface temperature and other oceanographic data are also being collected.

As the Fagatele Bay sanctuary undergoes its management plan review, considering its role in protecting living resources from exploitation and harm will be a priority. One of the most important areas for improvement is monitoring the levels and type of use of sanctuary resources. This may include remote video monitoring of the site for tracking both allowed and illegal uses. The sanctuary will be looking to the Samoan people to play a significant role in determining the future of fish and other marine life populations within American Samoa's territorial waters.

Maritime Archaeological Resources

Although no maritime archaeological artifacts have been identified in Fagatele Bay sanctuary, regulations prohibit the removal, damage, or disturbance of any historical or cultural resource within the boundaries of the sanctuary.

A diver surveys the reef at Fagatele Bay. *Photo: Kip Evans*

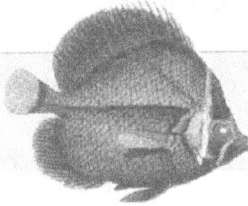

Concluding Remarks

Fagatele Bay National Marine Sanctuary is at an important period in its history. The sanctuary staff will soon begin a process to review its management plan. This opportunity will redefine the sanctuary's role and renew its place as a vital part of American Samoa's coastal and marine conservation efforts. It will also make the Fagatele Bay sanctuary a key component of the National Marine Sanctuary System's effort to better understand, protect and utilize the nation's marine environment.

Research and monitoring efforts in partnership with local and international researchers will continue to chart the path of Fagatele Bay's recovery and response to natural and human caused disruptions to its ecosystem. These studies will also help assess and guide future management actions designed to preserve the sanctuary's resources.

One of the most important aspects of the Fagatele Bay sanctuary is its location in American Samoa, where the Samoan people have a unique relationship to their land, sea and cultural traditions. Fagatele Bay can become part of this relationship by serving as a catalyst for revitalizing the bond between the Samoan people and their marine resources. For example, Samoan customs have been resilient to modern social change. This cultural resilience is exemplified in the tradition of "Sa" practiced by Samoan villages. It is a time of pause during the day for prayer and quiet reflection on how to improve their life and environment, indicating the high level of respect that American Samoa communities have for their traditions. Incorporating such practices into the management of Fagatele Bay could make the sanctuary a symbol of "fa'asamoa" (the Samoan way) of marine stewardship.

An American Samoa community practicing "Sa," a time when activities in the village stop for a period of reflection and prayer. Village men in maroon "lava lavas" stand along the road to signal passing vehicles to drive slowly and pedestrians to sit in respect of this tradition. This practice symbolizes the resiliency of Samoan culture. Fagatele Bay National Marine Sanctuary's place in American Samoa is also a symbol of this resilience by showing the "Samoan way" of respect and stewardship for their marine environment. Photo: Bill Kiene

Sunset at Fagatele Bay. *Photo: Kip Evans*

Acknowledgements

Clancy Environmental Consultants, Inc., under contract to NOAA, was instrumental in developing the template for this document and providing the initial material. We would particularly like to thank Jeff Rosen for developing the condition summary table and Karen Fox for drafting content. We thank our three reviewers for their helpful comments: Peter Craig, National Park of American Samoa; Charles Birkeland, Hawai'i Cooperative Fishery Research Unit; and Douglas Fenner, Department of Marine and Wildlife Resources.

References

Introduction
National Marine Sanctuary Program. 2004. A monitoring framework for the National Marine Sanctuary System. U.S. Dept. of Commerce, National Oceanic and Atmospheric Administration, National Ocean Service. Silver Spring, MD. 22 pp.

Overview
Fagatele Bay National Marine Sanctuary: About the Sanctuary
http://fagatelebay.noaa.gov/html/intro.html

Natural History Guide to American Samoa, P. Craig ed. 2nd edition 2005 96 pp. http://www.nps.gov/npsa/book/index.html

Site History and Resources
Geology
Final Environmental Impact Statement for the Proposed Fagatele Bay Sanctuary 1984 http://sanctuaries.noaa.gov/management/fr_notices.html

Fishery Ecosystem Plan for the American Samoa Archipelago 2005 http://www.wpcouncil.org/documents/FEPs/AmericanSamoaFEP/December12005AmericanSamoaFEP.pdf

Natural History Guide to American Samoa: Marine Environment http://www.nps.gov/npsa/book/index.htm

Commerce
American Samoa General Information Website
http://www.samoanet.com/amsamoa/

American Samoa Geographic Information System Users Group
http://doc.asg.as/

MBendi Website: http://www.mbendi.co.za/land/am/ao/p0005.htm

Water
U.S. Environmental Protection Agency: About Coral Reefs
http://www.epa.gov/owow/oceans/coral/about.html

Habitat
Fagatele Bay sanctuary GIS Data Archive
http://dusk2.geo.orst.edu/djl/samoa/

Mapping and GIS Capacity Building in American Samoa (Dawn Wright)
http://gis.esri.com/library/userconf/proc02/pap0101/p0101.htm

U.S. Geological Survey: U.S. Coral Reefs – Imperiled National Treasures
http://pubs.usgs.gov/fs/2002/fs025-02/

Western Pacific Fishery Management Council: Fishery Ecosystem Plan for the American Samoa Archipelego
http://www.wpcouncil.org/documents/FEPs/AmericanSamoaFEP/December12005AmericanSamoaFEP.pdf

Living Resources

Lamberts, A. E. 1983. An annotated check list of the corals of American Samoa. Atoll Research Bulletin 264: 1-19.

Mayor, A. 1924. Structure and ecology of Samoan reefs. Papers from the Department of Marine Biology, Carnegie Institution of Washington 19: 1-25, pl. 1-8

Moulton, M. P., J. G. Sanderson and R. F. Labisky. 2001. Patterns of success in game bird (Aves: Galliformes) introductions to the Hawaiian islands and New Zealand. Evolutionary Ecology Research 3: 507-519.

Mundy, C. 1996. A quantitative survey of the corals of American Samoa. Report to the Department of Marine and Wildlife Resources, PO Box 3730, Pago Pago, American Samoa. 96799, 24 pp.

NOAA: Pacific Fisheries Science Center. Ecological Assessment of Marine Invertebrates http://www.pifsc.noaa.gov/cred/inverts.php

Wass, R.C. 1982 Characterization of the inshore Samoan reef fish communities. Report to the Department of Marine and Wildlife Resources, PO Box 3730, Pago Pago, American Samoa. 96799, 48 pp

Maritime Archaeological Resources

Gould, R.A., Honor, KE and Reinhardt, J.K. 1985. Final project reports for Tutuila and Fagatele Bay prehistoric villages and Leone Bay petroglyphs. Brown University, Providence, RI.

Pressures

Crown-of-Thorns Outbreak

Changes in the Coral Reef Communities of Fagatele Bay National Marine Sanctuary and Tutuila Island 1982-1995 (C. Birkeland) http://www.fagatelebay.noaa.gov/html/docs/birkland_compiled95.pdf

Fagatele Bay National Marine Sanctuary: Research http://fagatelebay.noaa.gov/html/Research.html

Tropical Cyclones

Changes in the Coral Reef Communities of Fagatele Bay National Marine Sanctuary and Tutuila Island 1982-1995 (C. Birkeland) http://www.fagatelebay.noaa.gov/html/docs/birkland_compiled95.pdf

Elevated Ocean Temperature

Fagatele Bay National Marine Sanctuary: Research http://fagatelebay.noaa.gov/html/Research.html

Fenner, D. 2004. Summer coral bleaching event, 2004, on Tutuila, American Samoa. Report to Department of Marine and Wildlife Resources, American Samoa. 4 pp.

Goreau, T.J, Hayes, R.L. 1994. A survey of coral reef bleaching in the South Central Pacific during 1994. A report to the Coral Reef Initiative, U.S. Dept of State. 118 pp.

Natural History Guide to American Samoa (Marine Environment) http://www.nps.gov/npsa/book/index.htm

U.S. Geological Survey: U.S. Coral Reefs - Imperiled National Treasures http://pubs.usgs.gov/fs/2002/fs025-02/

Fishing

Fagatele Bay Dynamite Damage Assessment - June 5, 2005 http://sanctuaries.noaa.gov/visit/pdfs/dynamitedamage.pdf

Long Term Monitoring of Fagatele Bay sanctuary and Tutuila Island (American Samoa) 1985 to 2001: Summary of Surveys Conducted in 1998 and 2001"(C. Birkeland) http://fagatelebay.noaa.gov/html/docs/birkeland_report2001.pdf

Pacific Islands Fisheries Science Center http://www.pifsc.noaa.gov/wpacfin/as/Pages/as_data_menu.php

Page, M. 1998 The biology, community structure, growth and artisanal catch of parrotfishes of American Samoa. Report to the Department of Marine and Wildlife Resources, PO Box 3730, Pago Pago, American Samoa. 96799, 87 pp.

Western Pacific Fisheries Management Council http://www.wpcouncil.org/index.htm

Diseases

Coral Disease on the Reefs of American Samoa (Greta Aeby)

Status of Coral Reefs of the World 2004, Chapter 1: Global Threats http://www.aims.gov.au/pages/research/coral-bleaching/scr2004/pdf/scr2004v1-01.pdf

Work, T.M. and Rameyer, R.A. 2002. American Samoa Reef Health Survey. USGS-National Wildlife Health Center, Honolulu HI. 42 pp.

Agriculture

2003 and 2004 Statistical Yearbook of American Samoa http://www.spc.int/prism/country/as/stats/

Bruckner, A., K. Buja, L. Fairey, K. Gleason, M. Harmon, S. Heron, T. Hourigan, C. Jeffrey, J. Kellner, R. Kelty, B. Leeworthy, G. Liu, S. Pittman, A. Shapiro, A. Strong, J. Waddell, and P. Wiley. 2005. Environmental and Anthropogenic Threats to Coral Reef Ecosystems. pp. 12-44. The State of Coral Reef Ecosystems of the United States and Pacific Freely Associated States: 2005. NOAA Technical Memorandum NOS NCCOS 11. NOAA/NCCOS Center for Coastal Monitoring and Assessment's Biogeography Team. Silver Spring, MD. 522 pp. http://ccma.nos.noaa.gov/ecosystems/coralreef/coral_report_2005/Threats_Ch3_C.pdf

Economic Valuation of Coral Reefs and Adjacent Habitats in American Samoa, Final Report 2004 http://doc.asg.as/crag/ASCoralValuation04.pdf

Weed Mulch and No-Till Taro Cultivation in American Samoa (L. Hirata) http://www.agroecology.org/cases/notilltaro.htm

Visitation

Peter, C., G. DiDonato, D. Fenner and C. Hawkins. 2005. The State of Coral Reef Ecosystems of American Samoa. pp. 312-337. In: J. Waddell (ed.), The State of Coral Reef Ecosystems of the United States and Pacific Freely Associated States: 2005. NOAA Technical Memorandum NOS NCCOS 11. NOAA/NCCOS Center for Coastal Monitoring and Assessment's Biogeography Team. Silver Spring, MD. 522 pp. http://ccma.nos.noaa.gov/ecosystems/coralreef/coral_report_2005/AmSamoa_Ch11_C.pdf

Turgeon, D.D., R.G. Asch, B.D. Causey, R.E. Dodge, W. Jaap, K. Banks, J. Delaney, B.D. Keller, R. Speiler, C.A. Matos, J.R. Garcia, E. Diaz, D. Catanzaro, C.S. Rogers, Z. Hillis-Starr, R. Nemeth, M. Taylor, G.P. Schmahl, M.W. Miller, D.A. Gulko, J.E. Maragos, A.M. Friedlander, C.L. Hunter, R.S. Brainard, P. Craig, R.H. Richond, G. Davis, J. Starmer, M. Trianni, P. Houk, C.E. Birkeland, A. Edward, Y. Golbuu, J. Gutierrez, N. Idechong, G. Paulay, A. Tafileichig, and N. Vander Velde. 2002. The State of Coral Reef Ecosystems of the United States and Pacific Freely Associated States: 2002. National Oceanic and Atmospheric Administration/National Ocean Service/National Centers for Coastal Ocean Science, Silver Spring, MD. 265 pp. http://www.nccos.noaa.gov/documents/status_coralreef.pdf

State of Sanctuary Resources
Water
American Samoa Nonpoint Source Pollution Program FY05 Annual Report

DiDonato, G. 2004. Developing an initial watershed classification for American Samoa. Report to the American Samoa Environmental Protection Agency, PO Box PPA, Pago Pago, American Samoa, 96799. 12p.

Territory of American Samoa Integrated Water Quality Monitoring and Assessment Report 2004

Habitat
Birkeland, C., Randall, R. H., Green, A.L, Smith, B.D., Wilkins, S. 1997. Changes in the coral reef communities of Fagatele Bay National Marine Sanctuary and Tutuila Island (American Samoa) over the last two decades. Report to the National Oceanic and Atmospheric Administration, U.S. Department of Commerce, 225 pp.

Birkeland, C., Green, A., Mundy, C., Miller, K. 2004. Long term monitoring of Fagatele Bay National Marine Sanctuary and Tutuila Island (American Samoa) 1985 to 2001: summary of surveys conducted in 1998 and 2001. Report to the National Oceanic and Atmospheric Administration, U.S. Department of Commerce, 158 pp.Green, A. 2002. Status of the coral reefs on the main volcanic islands of American Samoa: a resurvey of long term monitoring sites (benthic communities, fish communities, and key macroinvertebrates). Report to DMWR.

Green, A. 2002. Status of the coral reefs on the main volcanic islands of American Samoa: a resurvey of long term monitoring sites (benthic communities, fish communities, and key macroinvertebrates). Report to DMWR.

Green, A., Miller, K. and Mundy, C. 2005. Long term monitoring of Fagatele Bay National Marine Sanctuary. Tutuila Island, American Samoa: results of surveys conducted in 2004, including a resurvey of the historic Aua transect. Report to US Department of Commerce and American Samoa Government. 93 pp.

Houk, P., Didonato, G., Iguel, J., and Van Woesik, R.: 2005, Assessing the effects of non-point source pollution on American Samoa's coral reef communities, Env. Mon. Ass. 107, 11-27.

Peter, C., G. DiDonato, D. Fenner and C. Hawkins. 2005. The State of Coral Reef Ecosystems of American Samoa. pp. 312-337. In: J. Waddell (ed.), The State of Coral Reef Ecosystems of the United States and

Pacific Freely Associated States: 2005. NOAA Technical Memorandum NOS NCCOS 11. NOAA/NCCOS Center for Coastal Monitoring and Assessment's Biogeography Team. Silver Spring, MD. 522 pp. http://ccma.nos.noaa.gov/ecosystems/coralreef/coral_report_2005/AmSamoa_Ch11_C.pdf

Whaylen, L. and Fenner, D. 2005. Report of 2005 American Samoa Coral Reef Monitoring Program. Report to Department of Marine and Wildlife Resources and Coral Reef Advisory Group. 40 pp.

Living Resources – Coral Reefs
Birkeland, C., Randall, R., Amesbury, S.S. 1985. Coral and reef-fish assessment of the Fagatele Bay National Marine Sanctuary. Report to NOAA. 126 pp.

Birkeland, C., Randall, R., Wass, R., Smith, B, Wilkens, S. 1987. Biological resource assessment of the Fagatele Bay National Marine Sanctuary. NOAA Technical Memorandum NOS MEMD 3. 232 pp.

Birkeland, C., Randall, R., Amesbury, S. 1991. Coral and reef-fish assessment of the Fagatele Bay National Marine Sanctuary. Report to the National Oceanic and Atmospheric Administration U.S. Department of Commerce. 126 pp.

Birkeland, C., Randall, R. H., Green, A.L, Smith, B.D., Wilkins, S. 1996. Changes in the coral reef communities of Fagatele Bay National Marine Sanctuary and Tutuila Island (American Samoa) over the last two decades. Report to the National Oceanic and Atmospheric Administration, U.S. Department of Commerce, 225 pp.

Birkeland, C., Belliaveau, S.A. 2000. Resurvey of the Aua Transect After the Ship Removal. Report to the National Oceanic and Atmospheric Administration U.S. Department of Commerce. 2 pp.

Birkeland, C., Randall, R.H., Green, A.L., Smith, B.D., Wilkins, S. 2003. Changes in the coral reef communities of Fagatele Bay National Marine Sanctuary and Tutuila Island (American Samoa), 1982-1995. Fagatele Bay National Marine Sanctuary Science Series 2003-1.

Birkeland, C., Green, A., Mundy, C., Miller, K. 2004. Long term monitoring of Fagatele Bay National Marine Sanctuary and Tutuila Island (American Samoa) 1985 to 2001: summary of surveys conducted in 1998 and 2001. Report to the National Oceanic and Atmospheric Administration, U.S. Department of Commerce, 158 pp.

Coles, S.L., Reath, P.R., Skelton P.A., Bonito,V., DeFelice R.C., Basch, L. 2003. Introduced marine species in Pago Pago Harbor, Fagatele Bay and the National Park Coast, American Samoa. Bishp Museum Technical Report No 26, Honlolulu HI, 182 pp.

Craig, P. 2005. Natural History Guide to American Samoa http://www.nps.gov/npsa/book/index.htm

Dahl, A.L., Lamberts, A.E. 1977. Environmental impact on a Samoan Coral Reef: a resurvey of Mayor's 1917 transect. Pacific Science 31: 209-319.

Fisk, D., Birkeland, C. 2002 Status of coral communities in American Samoa. A re-survey of long-term monitoring sites. Report to the Department of Marine and Wildlife Resources, PO Box 3730, Pago Pago, American Samoa. 96799, 134pp.

Green, A.L. 1996. Status of the coral reefs of the Samoan Archipelago Report to the Department of Marine and Wildlife Resources, PO Box 3730, Pago Pago, American Samoa. 96799, 120pp

Green, A.L., Birkeland, C.E., Randall, R.H., Smith, B.D., Wilkins, S. 1997. 78 years of coral reef degradation in Pago Pago Harbour: a quantitative record. Proc. 8th Int Coral Reef Sym 2: 1883-1888.

Green, A.L., Birkeland, C.E., Randall, R.H. 1999 Twenty years of disturbance and change in Fagatele Bay National Marine Sanctuary, American Samoa. Pacific Science 53(4): 376- 400.

Green, A. 2002. Status of the coral reefs on the main volcanic islands of American Samoa: a resurvey of long term monitoring sites (benthic communities, fish communities, and key macroinvertebrates). Report to DMWR.

Green, A., Miller, K. and Mundy, C. 2005. Long term monitoring of Fagatele Bay National Marine Sanctuary. Tutuila Island, American Samoa: results of surveys conducted in 2004, including a resurvey of the historic Aua transect. Report to US Department of Commerce and American Samoa Government. 93 pp.

McCardle, B. 2003. Report: Statistical analyses for Coral Reef Advisory Group. 142 pp.

Peter, C., G. DiDonato, D. Fenner and C. Hawkins. 2005. The State of Coral Reef Ecosystems of American Samoa. pp. 312-337. In: J. Waddell (ed.), The State of Coral Reef Ecosystems of the United States and Pacific Freely Associated States: 2005. NOAA Technical Memorandum NOS NCCOS 11. NOAA/NCCOS Center for Coastal Monitoring and Assessment's Biogeography Team. Silver Spring, MD. 522 pp. http://ccma.nos.noaa.gov/ecosystems/coralreef/coral_report_2005/AmSamoa_Ch11_C.pdf

Whaylen, L. and Fenner, D. 2005. Report of 2005 American Samoa Coral Reef Monitoring Program. Report to Department of Marine and Wildlife Resources and Coral Reef Advisory Group. 40 pp.

Living Resources – Sea Turtles
Craig, P. 2005. Natural History Guide to American Samoa http://www.nps.gov/npsa/book/index.htm

Peter, C., G. DiDonato, D. Fenner and C. Hawkins. 2005. The State of Coral Reef Ecosystems of American Samoa. pp. 312-337. In: J. Waddell (ed.), The State of Coral Reef Ecosystems of the United States and Pacific Freely Associated States: 2005. NOAA Technical Memorandum NOS NCCOS 11. NOAA/NCCOS Center for Coastal Monitoring and Assessment's Biogeography Team. Silver Spring, MD. 522 pp. http://ccma.nos.noaa.gov/ecosystems/coralreef/coral_report_2005/AmSamoa_Ch11_C.pdf

Living Resources – Marine Mammals
Peter, C., G. DiDonato, D. Fenner and C. Hawkins. 2005. The State of Coral Reef Ecosystems of American Samoa. pp. 312-337. In: J. Waddell (ed.), The State of Coral Reef Ecosystems of the United States and Pacific Freely Associated States: 2005. NOAA Technical Memorandum NOS NCCOS 11. NOAA/NCCOS Center for Coastal Monitoring and Assessment's Biogeography Team. Silver Spring, MD. 522 pp. http://ccma.nos.noaa.gov/ecosystems/coralreef/coral_report_2005/AmSamoa_Ch11_C.pdf

Response to Pressures
General
American Samoa's Coral Reef Initiative: Coral Reef Advisory Group (CRAG) http://doc.asg.as/CRAG/Default.htm

Fagatele Bay National Marine Sanctuary Regulations, Federal Register, Vol 51, No 82 April 29 1986, p 15878 - 15883

Final Environmental Impact Statement and Management Plan for the proposed Fagatele Bay National Marine Sanctuary 1984. NOAA Sanctuary Programs Division, Washington DC and Development Planning Office, American Samoa.

NOAA Coral Reef Conservation Program: Coral Reef Conservation Act http://www.coralreef.noaa.gov/

Water
Fagatele Bay National Marine Sanctuary: Resource Management http://fagatelebay.noaa.gov/html/management.html

Partnerships in Monitoring: A Water Quality Example from American Samoa http://www.nature.nps.gov/im/units/secn/Downloads/asemap.pdf

Peshut, P. 2003 Monitoring demonstrates management success to improve water quality in Pago Pago Harbor, American Samoa. In: Wilkinson, C., Green, A., Almany, J., Dionne, S. Monitoring Coral Reef Marine Protected Areas. A Practical Guide on How Monitoring Can Support Effective Management of MPAs. Australian Institute of Marine Science and the IUCN Marine Program, Townsville, Australia, 68 pp.

U.S. Environmental Protection Agency Water Quality Standards http://www.epa.gov/waterscience/standards/wqslibrary/territories/american_samoa_9_wqs.pdf

Habitat
Fagatele Bay National Marine Sanctuary: Resource Management http://fagatelebay.noaa.gov/html/management.html

Living Resources
American Samoa GIS User Group http://doc.asg.as

Endangered Species Act of 1973 http://www.nmfs.noaa.gov/pr/laws/esa.htm

Fagatele Bay National Marine Sanctuary GIS Data Archive http://dusk2.geo.orst.edu/djl/samoa/

Fagatele Bay National Marine Sanctuary: Research http://fagatelebay.noaa.gov/html/research.html

Fagatele Bay National Marine Sanctuary: Resource Management http://fagatelebay.noaa.gov/html/management.html

Guide to the Laws and Treaties of the United States for Protecting Migratory Birds http://www.fws.gov/migratorybirds/intrnltr/treatlaw.html

Marine Mammal Protection Act of 1972 http://www.nmfs.noaa.gov/pr/laws/mmpa.htm

Pacific Islands Fisheries Science Center http://www.pifsc.noaa.gov/cred/

Pacific Islands Fisheries Science Center, Real-time water temperature
data: http://crei.pifsc.noaa.gov/ocean_data.html

Saucerman, S. 1995. Assessing the management needs of a coral reef
fishery in decline. South Pacific Commission, Joint FFA/SPC workshop
on the management of South Pacific inshore fisheries, Noumea,
New Caledonia 26 June-7 July 1995)

Maritime Archaeological Resources
Fagatele Bay National Marine Sanctuary: Resource Management
http://fagatelebay.noaa.gov/html/management.htm

Additional Resources

American Samoa Department of Commerce
http://www.asdoc.info/index.htm

American Samoa Government
http://www.asg-gov.net/index.htm

Fagatele Bay National Marine Sanctuary
http://fagatelebay.noaa.gov/

Fagatele Bay National Marine Sanctuary GIS Data Archive
http://dusk2.geo.orst.edu/djl/samoa/

Marine Protected Areas of the United States
http://www.mpa.gov/

NOAA Coral Reef Conservation Program
http://www.coralreef.noaa.gov/

NOAA National Marine Sanctuary Program
http://www.sanctuaries.nos.noaa.gov/welcome.html

NOAA's National Marine Fisheries Service
http://www.nmfs.noaa.gov/

NOAA Ocean Explorer
http://www.oceanexplorer.noaa.gov/welcome.html

National Park Service: National Park of American Samoa
http://www.nps.gov/npsa/

Western Pacific Fishery Management Council
http://www.wpcouncil.org/

Woods Hole Oceanographic Institution
http://www.whoi.edu/

Appendix A: Rating Scheme for System-Wide Monitoring Questions

The purpose of this appendix is to clarify the 17 questions and possible responses used to report the condition of sanctuary resources in "Condition Reports" for all national marine sanctuaries. Individual staff and partners utilized this guidance, as well as their own informed and detailed understanding of the site to make judgments about the status and trends of sanctuary resources.

The questions derive from the National Marine Sanctuary Program mission, and a system-wide monitoring framework (National Marine Sanctuary Program, 2004) developed to ensure the timely flow of data and information to those responsible for managing and protecting resources in the ocean and coastal zone, and to those that use, depend on, and study the ecosystems encompassed by the sanctuaries. They are being used to guide staff and partners at each of the 14 sites in the sanctuary system in the development of this first periodic sanctuary condition report. The questions are meant to set the limits of judgments so that responses can be confined to certain reporting categories that will later be compared among all sites, and combined.

Following a brief discussion about each question, statements are presented that were used to judge the status and assign a corresponding color code. These statements are customized for each question. In addition, the following options are available for all questions: " N/A" - the question does not apply; and "Undet." - resource status is undetermined.

Symbols used to indicate trends are the same for all questions: "▲" - conditions appear to be improving; "▬" - conditions do not appear to be changing; "▼" - conditions appear to be declining; and "?" – trend is undetermined.

Water Stressors	1. Are specific or multiple stressors, including changing oceanographic and atmospheric conditions, affecting water quality and how are they changing?

This is meant to capture shifts in condition arising from certain changing physical processes and anthropogenic inputs. Factors resulting in regionally accelerated rates of change in water temperature, salinity, dissolved oxygen, or water clarity, could all be judged to reduce water quality. Localized changes in circulation or sedimentation resulting, for example, from coastal construction or dredge spoil disposal, can affect light penetration, salinity regimes, oxygen levels, productivity, waste transport, and other factors that influence habitat and living resource quality. Human inputs, generally in the form of contaminants from point or non-point sources, including fertilizers, pesticides, hydrocarbons, heavy metals, and sewage, are common causes of environmental degradation, often in combination rather than alone. Certain biotoxins, such as domoic acid, may be of particular interest to specific sanctuaries. When present in the water column, any of these contaminants can affect marine life by direct contact or ingestion, or through bioaccumulation via the food chain.

[Note: Over time, accumulation in sediments can sequester and concentrate contaminants. Their effects may manifest only when the sediments are resuspended during storm or other energetic events. In such cases, reports of status should be made under Question 7 – Habitat contaminants.]

Good	Conditions do not appear to have the potential to negatively affect living resources or habitat quality.
Good/Fair	Selected conditions may preclude full development of living resource assemblages and habitats, but are not likely to cause substantial or persistent declines.
Fair	Selected conditions may inhibit the development of assemblages, and may cause measurable but not severe declines in living resources and habitats.
Fair/Poor	Selected conditions have caused or are likely to cause severe declines in some but not all living resources and habitats.
Poor	Selected conditions have caused or are likely to cause severe declines in most if not all living resources and habitats.

Eutrophic Condition

2. What is the eutrophic condition of sanctuary waters and how is it changing?

Nutrient enrichment often leads to planktonic and/or benthic algae blooms. Some affect benthic communities directly through space competition. Overgrowth and other competitive interactions (e.g., accumulation of algal-sediment mats) often lead to shifts in dominance in the benthic assemblage. Disease incidence and frequency can also be affected by algae competition and the resulting chemistry along competitive boundaries. Blooms can also affect water column conditions, including light penetration and plankton availability, which can alter pelagic food webs. Harmful algal blooms often affect resources, as biotoxins are released into the water and air, and oxygen can be depleted.

Good	Conditions do not appear to have the potential to negatively affect living resources or habitat quality.
Good/Fair	Selected conditions may preclude full development of living resource assemblages and habitats, but are not likely to cause substantial or persistent declines.
Fair	Selected conditions may inhibit the development of assemblages, and may cause measurable but not severe declines in living resources and habitats.
Fair/Poor	Selected conditions have caused or are likely to cause severe declines in some but not all living resources and habitats.
Poor	Selected conditions have caused or are likely to cause severe declines in most if not all living resources and habitats.

Human Health

3. Do sanctuary waters pose risks to human health and how are they changing?

Human health concerns are generally aroused by evidence of contamination (usually bacterial or chemical) in bathing waters or fish intended for consumption. They also emerge when harmful algal blooms are reported or when cases of respiratory distress or other disorders attributable to harmful algal blooms increase dramatically. Any of these conditions should be considered in the course of judging the risk to humans posed by waters in a marine sanctuary.

Some sites may have access to specific information on beach and shellfish conditions. In particular, beaches may be closed when criteria for safe water body contact are exceeded, or shellfish harvesting may be prohibited when contaminant loads or infection rates exceed certain levels. These conditions can be evaluated in the context of the descriptions below.

Good	Conditions do not appear to have the potential to negatively affect human health.
Good/Fair	Selected conditions that have the potential to affect human health may exist but human impacts have not been reported.
Fair	Selected conditions have resulted in isolated human impacts, but evidence does not justify widespread or persistent concern.
Fair/Poor	Selected conditions have caused or are likely to cause severe impacts, but cases to date have not suggested a pervasive problem.
Poor	Selected conditions warrant widespread concern and action, as large-scale, persistent, and/or repeated severe impacts are likely or have occurred.

Water
Human Activities

4. What are the levels of human activities that may influence water quality and how are they changing?

Among the human activities in or near sanctuaries that affect water quality are those involving direct discharges (transiting vessels, visiting vessels, onshore and offshore industrial facilities, public wastewater facilities), those that contribute contaminants to stream, river, and water control discharges (agriculture, runoff from impermeable surfaces through storm drains, conversion of land use), and those releasing airborne chemicals that subsequently deposit via particulates at sea (vessels, land-based traffic, power plants, manufacturing facilities, refineries). In addition, dredging and trawling can cause resuspension of contaminants in sediments.

Good	Few or no activities occur that are likely to negatively affect water quality.
Good/Fair	Some potentially harmful activities exist, but they do not appear to have had a negative effect on water quality.
Fair	Selected activities have resulted in measurable resource impacts, but evidence suggests effects are localized, not widespread.
Fair/Poor	Selected activities have caused or are likely to cause severe impacts, and cases to date suggest a pervasive problem.
Poor	Selected activities warrant widespread concern and action, as large-scale, persistent, and/or repeated severe impacts have occurred or are likely to occur.

Habitat
Abundance & Distribution

5. What are the abundance and distribution of major habitat types and how are they changing?

Habitat loss is of paramount concern when it comes to protecting marine and terrestrial ecosystems. Of greatest concern to sanctuaries are changes caused, either directly or indirectly, by human activities. The loss of shoreline is recognized as a problem indirectly caused by human activities. Habitats with submerged aquatic vegetation are often altered by changes in water conditions in estuaries, bays, and nearshore waters. Intertidal zones can be affected for long periods by spills or by chronic pollutant exposure. Beaches and haul-out areas can be littered with dangerous marine debris, as can the water column or benthic habitats. Sandy subtidal areas and hardbottoms are frequently disturbed or destroyed by trawling. Even rocky areas several hundred meters deep are increasingly affected by certain types of trawls, bottom longlines, and fish traps. Groundings, anchors, and divers damage submerged reefs. Cables and pipelines disturb corridors across numerous habitat types and can be destructive if they become mobile. Shellfish dredging removes, alters, and fragments habitats.

The result of these activities is the gradual reduction of the extent and quality of marine habitats. Losses can often be quantified through visual surveys and to some extent using high-resolution mapping. This question asks about the quality of habitats compared to those that would be expected without human impacts. The status depends on comparison to a baseline that existed in the past—one toward which restoration efforts might aim.

Good	Habitats are in pristine or near-pristine condition and are unlikely to preclude full community development.
Good/Fair	Selected habitat loss or alteration has taken place, precluding full development of living resources assemblages, but it is unlikely to cause substantial or persistent degradation in living resources or water quality.
Fair	Selected habitat loss or alteration may inhibit the development of assemblages, and may cause measurable, but not severe declines in living resources or water quality.
Fair/Poor	Selected habitat loss or alteration has caused or is likely to cause severe declines in some but not all living resources or water quality.
Poor	Selected habitat loss or alteration has caused or is likely to cause severe declines in most if not all living resources or water quality.

Habitat
Structure

6. What is the condition of biologically structured habitats and how is it changing?

Many organisms depend on the integrity of their habitats and that integrity is largely determined by the condition of particular living organisms. Coral reefs may be the best known examples of such biologically structured habitats. Not only is the substrate itself biogenic, but the diverse assemblages residing within and on the reefs depend on and interact with each other in tightly linked food webs. They also depend on each other for the recycling of wastes, hygiene, and the maintenance of water quality, among other requirements.

Kelp beds may not be biogenic habitats to the extent of coral reefs, but kelp provides essential habitat for assemblages that would not reside or function together without it. There are other communities of organisms that are also similarly co-dependent, such as hard-bottom communities, which may be structured by bivalves, octocorals, coralline algae, or other groups that generate essential habitat for other species. Intertidal assemblages structured by mussels, barnacles, and algae are another example, seagrass beds another.

This question is intended to address these types of places, where organisms form structures (habitats) on which other organisms depend.

Good	Habitats are in pristine or near-pristine condition and are unlikely to preclude full community development.
Good/Fair	Selected habitat loss or alteration has taken place, precluding full development of living resources, but it is unlikely to cause substantial or persistent degradation in living resources or water quality.
Fair	Selected habitat loss or alteration may inhibit the development of living resources, and may cause measurable but not severe declines in living resources or water quality.
Fair/Poor	Selected habitat loss or alteration has caused or is likely to cause severe declines in some but not all living resources or water quality.
Poor	Selected habitat loss or alteration has caused or is likely to cause severe declines in most if not all living resources or water quality.

Habitat
Contaminants

7. What are the contaminant concentrations in sanctuary habitats and how are they changing?

This question addresses the need to understand the risk posed by contaminants within benthic formations, such as soft sediments, hard bottoms, or biogenic organisms. In the first two cases, the contaminants can become available when released via disturbance. They can also pass upwards through the food chain after being ingested by bottom dwelling prey species. The contaminants of concern generally include pesticides, hydrocarbons, and heavy metals, but the specific concerns of individual sanctuaries may differ substantially.

Good	Contaminants do not appear to have the potential to negatively affect living resources or water quality.
Good/Fair	Selected contaminants may preclude full development of living resource assemblages, but are not likely to cause substantial or persistent degradation.
Fair	Selected contaminants may inhibit the development of assemblages, and may cause measurable but not severe declines in living resources or water quality.
Fair/Poor	Selected contaminants have caused or are likely to cause severe declines in some but not all living resources or water quality.
Poor	Selected contaminants have caused or are likely to cause severe declines in most if not all living resources or water quality.

Habitat
Human Activities

8. What are the levels of human activities that may influence habitat quality and how are they changing?

Human activities that degrade habitat quality do so by affecting structural (geological), biological, oceanographic, acoustic, or chemical characteristics. Structural impacts include removal or mechanical alteration, including various fishing techniques (trawls, traps, dredges, longlines, and even hook-and-line in some habitats), dredging channels and harbors and dumping spoil, vessel groundings, anchoring, laying pipelines and cables, installing offshore structures, discharging drill cuttings, dragging tow cables, and placing artificial reefs. Removal or alteration of critical biological components of habitats can occur along with several of the above activities, most notably trawling, groundings, and cable drags. Marine debris, particularly in large quantities (e.g., lost gill nets and other types of fishing gear), can affect both biological and structural habitat components. Changes in water circulation often occur when channels are dredged, fill is added, coastal areas are reinforced, or other construction takes place. These activities affect habitat by changing food delivery, waste removal, water quality (e.g., salinity, clarity and sedimentation), recruitment patterns, and a host of other factors. Acoustic impacts can occur to water column habitats and organisms from acute and chronic sources of anthropogenic noise (e.g., shipping, boating, construction). Chemical alterations most commonly occur following spills and can have both acute and chronic impacts.

Good	Few or no activities occur that are likely to negatively affect habitat quality.
Good/Fair	Some potentially harmful activities exist, but they do not appear to have had a negative effect on habitat quality.
Fair	Selected activities have resulted in measurable habitat impacts, but evidence suggests effects are localized, not widespread.
Fair/Poor	Selected activities have caused or are likely to cause severe impacts, and cases to date suggest a pervasive problem.
Poor	Selected activities warrant widespread concern and action, as large-scale, persistent, and/or repeated severe impacts have occurred or are likely to occur.

Living Resources
Biodiversity

9. What is the status of biodiversity and how is it changing?

This is intended to elicit thought and assessment of the condition of living resources based on expected biodiversity levels and the interactions between species. Intact ecosystems require that all parts not only exist, but that they function together, resulting in natural symbioses, competition, and predator-prey relationships. Community integrity, resistance and resilience all depend on these relationships. Abundance, relative abundance, trophic structure, richness, H' diversity, evenness, and other measures are often used to assess these attributes.

Good	Biodiversity appears to reflect pristine or near-pristine conditions and promotes ecosystem integrity (full community development and function).
Good/Fair	Selected biodiversity loss has taken place, precluding full community development and function, but it is unlikely to cause substantial or persistent degradation of ecosystem integrity.
Fair	Selected biodiversity loss may inhibit full community development and function, and may cause measurable but not severe degradation of ecosystem integrity.
Fair/Poor	Selected biodiversity loss has caused or is likely to cause severe declines in some but not all ecosystem components and reduce ecosystem integrity.
Poor	Selected biodiversity loss has caused or is likely to cause severe declines in ecosystem integrity.

Living Resources
Extracted Species

10. What is the status of environmentally sustainable fishing and how is it changing?

Commercial and recreational harvesting are highly selective activities, for which fishers and collectors target a limited number of species, and often remove high proportions of populations. In addition to removing significant amounts of biomass from the ecosystem, reducing its availability to other consumers, these activities tend to disrupt specific and often critical food web links. When too much extraction occurs (i.e. ecologically unsustainable harvesting), trophic cascades ensue, resulting in changes in the abundance of non-targeted species as well. It also reduces the ability of the targeted species to replenish populations at a rate that supports continued ecosystem integrity.

It is essential to understand whether removals are occurring at ecologically sustainable levels. Knowing extraction levels and determining the impacts of removal are both ways that help gain this understanding. Measures for target species of abundance, catch amounts or rates (e.g., catch per unit effort), trophic structure, and changes in non-target species abundance are all generally used to assess these conditions.

Other issues related to this question include whether fishers are using gear that is compatible with the habitats being fished and whether that gear minimizes by-catch and incidental take of marine mammals. For example, bottom-tending gear often destroys or alters both benthic structure and non-targeted animal and plant communities. "Ghost fishing" occurs when lost traps continue to capture organisms. Lost or active nets, as well as lines used to mark and tend traps and other fishing gear, can entangle marine mammals. Any of these could be considered indications of environmentally unsustainable fishing techniques.

Good	Extraction does not appear to affect ecosystem integrity (full community development and function).
Good/Fair	Extraction takes place, precluding full community development and function, but it is unlikely to cause substantial or persistent degradation of ecosystem integrity.
Fair	Extraction may inhibit full community development and function, and may cause measurable but not severe degradation of ecosystem integrity.
Fair/Poor	Extraction has caused or is likely to cause severe declines in some but not all ecosystem components and reduce ecosystem integrity.
Poor	Extraction has caused or is likely to cause severe declines in ecosystem integrity.

Living Resources
Invasive Species

11. What is the status of non-indigenous species and how is it changing?

Non-indigenous species are generally considered problematic, and candidates for rapid response, if found, soon after invasion. For those that become established, their impacts can sometimes be assessed by quantifying changes in the affected native species. This question allows sanctuaries to report on the threat posed by non-indigenous species. In some cases, the presence of a species alone constitutes a significant threat (certain invasive algae). In other cases, impacts have been measured, and may or may not significantly affect ecosystem integrity.

Good	Non-indigenous species are not suspected or do not appear to affect ecosystem integrity (full community development and function).
Good/Fair	Non-indigenous species exist, precluding full community development and function, but are unlikely to cause substantial or persistent degradation of ecosystem integrity.
Fair	Non-indigenous species may inhibit full community development and function, and may cause measurable but not severe degradation of ecosystem integrity.
Fair/Poor	Non-indigenous species have caused or are likely to cause severe declines in some but not all ecosystem components and reduce ecosystem integrity.
Poor	Non-indigenous species have caused or are likely to cause severe declines in ecosystem integrity.

Living Resources
Key Species

12. What is the status of key species and how is it changing?

Certain species can be defined as "key" within a marine sanctuary. Some might be keystone species, that is, species on which the persistence of a large number of other species in the ecosystem depends—the pillar of community stability. Their functional contribution to ecosystem function is disproportionate to their numerical abundance or biomass and their impact is therefore important at the community or ecosystem level. Their removal initiates changes in ecosystem structure and sometimes the disappearance of or dramatic increase in the abundance of dependent species. Keystone species may include certain habitat modifiers, predators, herbivores, and those involved in critical symbiotic relationships (e.g. cleaning or co-habitating species).

Other key species may include those that are indicators of ecosystem condition or change (e.g., particularly sensitive species), those targeted for special protection efforts, or charismatic species that are identified with certain areas or ecosystems. These may or may not meet the definition of keystone, but do require assessments of status and trends.

Good	Key and keystone species appear to reflect pristine or near-pristine conditions and may promote ecosystem integrity (full community development and function).
Good/Fair	Selected key or keystone species are at reduced levels, perhaps precluding full community development and function, but substantial or persistent declines are not expected.
Fair	The reduced abundance of selected keystone species may inhibit full community development and function, and may cause measurable but not severe degradation of ecosystem integrity; or selected key species are at reduced levels, but recovery is possible.
Fair/Poor	The reduced abundance of selected keystone species has caused or is likely to cause severe declines in some but not all ecosystem components, and reduce ecosystem integrity; or selected key species are at substantially reduced levels, and prospects for recovery are uncertain.
Poor	The reduced abundance of selected keystone species has caused or is likely to cause severe declines in ecosystem integrity; or selected key species are a severely reduced levels, and recovery is unlikely.

Living Resources
Health of Key Species

13. What is the condition or health of key species and how is it changing?

For those species considered essential to ecosystem integrity, measures of their condition can be important to determining the likelihood that they will persist and continue to provide vital ecosystem functions. Measures of condition may include growth rates, fecundity, recruitment, age-specific survival, tissue contaminant levels, pathologies (disease incidence tumors, deformities), the presence and abundance of critical symbionts, or parasite loads. Similar measures of condition may also be appropriate for other key species (indicator, protected, or charismatic species). In contrast to the question about keystone species (#12 above), the impact of changes in the abundance or condition of key species is more likely to be observed at the population or individual level, and less likely to result in ecosystem or community effects.

Good	The condition of key resources appears to reflect pristine or near-pristine conditions.
Good/Fair	The condition of selected key resources is not optimal, perhaps precluding full ecological function, but substantial or persistent declines are not expected.
Fair	The diminished condition of selected key resources may cause a measurable but not severe reduction in ecological function, but recovery is possible.
Fair/Poor	The comparatively poor condition of selected key resources makes prospects for recovery uncertain.
Poor	The poor condition of selected key resources makes recovery unlikely.

Living Resources
Human Activities

14. What are the levels of human activities that may influence living resource quality and how are they changing?

Human activities that degrade living resource quality do so by causing a loss or reduction of one or more species, by disrupting critical life stages, by impairing various physiological processes, or by promoting the introduction of non-indigenous species or pathogens. (Note: Activities that impact habitat and water quality may also affect living resources. These activities are dealt with in Questions 4 and 8, and many are repeated here as they also have direct effect on living resources).

Fishing and collecting are the primary means of removing resources. Bottom trawling, seine-fishing, and the collection of ornamental species for the aquarium trade are all common examples, some being more selective than others. Chronic mortality can be caused by marine debris derived from commercial or recreational vessel traffic, lost fishing gear, and excess visitation, resulting in the gradual loss of some species.

Critical life stages can be affected in various ways. Mortality to adult stages is often caused by trawling and other fishing techniques, cable drags, dumping spoil or drill cuttings, vessel groundings, or persistent anchoring. Contamination of areas by acute or chronic spills, discharges by vessels, or municipal and industrial facilities can make them unsuitable for recruitment; the same activities can make nursery habitats unsuitable. Although coastal armoring and construction can increase the availability of surfaces suitable for the recruitment and growth of hard bottom species, the activity may disrupt recruitment patterns for other species (e.g., intertidal soft bottom animals) and habitat may be lost.

Spills, discharges, and contaminants released from sediments (e.g., by dredging and dumping) can all cause physiological impairment and tissue contamination. Such activities can affect all life stages by reducing fecundity, increasing larval, juvenile, and adult mortality, reducing disease resistance, and increasing susceptibility to predation. Bioaccumulation allows some contaminants to move upward through the food chain, disproportionately affecting certain species.

Activities that promote introductions include bilge discharges and ballast water exchange, commercial shipping and vessel transportation. Releases of aquarium fish can also lead to species introductions.

Good	Few or no activities occur that are likely to negatively affect living resource quality.
Good/Fair	Some potentially harmful activities exist, but they do not appear to have had a negative effect on living resource quality.
Fair	Selected activities have resulted in measurable living resource impacts, but evidence suggests effects are localized, not widespread.
Fair/Poor	Selected activities have caused or are likely to cause severe impacts, and cases to date suggest a pervasive problem.
Poor	Selected activities warrant widespread concern and action, as large-scale, persistent, and/or repeated severe impacts have occurred or are likely to occur.

Maritime Archaeological Resources
Integrity

15. What is the integrity of known maritime archaeological resources and how is it changing?

The condition of archaeological resources in a marine sanctuary significantly affects their value for science and education, as well as the resource's eligibility for listing in the National Register of Historic Places. Assessments of archaeological sites include evaluation of the apparent levels of site integrity, which are based on levels of previous human disturbance and the level of natural deterioration. The historical, scientific and educational values of sites are also evaluated, and are substantially determined and affected by site condition.

Good	Known archaeological resources appear to reflect little or no unexpected disturbance.
Good/Fair	Selected archaeological resources exhibit indications of disturbance, but there appears to have been little or no reduction in historical, scientific, or educational value.
Fair	The diminished condition of selected archaeological resources has reduced, to some extent, their historical, scientific, or educational value, and may affect the eligibility of some sites for listing in the National Register of Historic Places.
Fair/Poor	The diminished condition of selected archaeological resources has substantially reduced their historical, scientific, or educational value, and is likely to affect their eligibility for listing in the National Register of Historic Places.
Poor	The degraded condition of known archaeological resources in general makes them ineffective in terms of historical, scientific, or educational value, and precludes their listing in the National Register of Historic Places.

Maritime Archaeological Resources
Threat to Environment

16. Do known maritime archaeological resources pose an environmental hazard and is this threat changing?

The sinking of a ship potentially introduces hazardous materials into the marine environment. This danger is true for historic shipwrecks as well. The issue is complicated by the fact that shipwrecks older than 50 years may be considered historical resources and must, by federal mandate, be protected. Many historic shipwrecks, particularly early to mid-20th century, still have the potential to retain oil and fuel in tanks and bunkers. As shipwrecks age and deteriorate, the potential for release of these materials into the environment increases.

Good	Known maritime archaeological resources pose few or no environmental threats.
Good/Fair	Selected maritime archaeological resources may pose isolated or limited environmental threats, but substantial or persistent impacts are not expected.
Fair	Selected maritime archaeological resources may cause measurable, but not severe impacts to certain sanctuary resources or areas, but recovery is possible.
Fair/Poor	Selected maritime archaeological resources pose substantial threats to certain sanctuary resources or areas, and prospects for recovery are uncertain.
Poor	Selected maritime archaeological resources pose serious threats to sanctuary resources, and recovery is unlikely.

Maritime Archaeological Resources
Human Activities

17. What are the levels of human activities that may influence maritime archaeological resource quality and how are they changing?

Some human maritime activities threaten the physical integrity of submerged archaeological resources. Archaeological site integrity is compromised when elements are moved, removed, or otherwise damaged. Threats come from looting by divers, inadvertent damage by scuba diving visitors, improperly conducted archaeology that does not fully document site disturbance, anchoring, groundings, and commercial and recreational fishing activities, among others.

Good	Few or no activities occur that are likely to negatively affect maritime archaeological resource integrity.
Good/Fair	Some potentially relevant activities exist, but they do not appear to have had a negative effect on maritime archaeological resource integrity.
Fair	Selected activities have resulted in measurable impacts to maritime archaeological resources, but evidence suggests effects are localized, not widespread.
Fair/Poor	Selected activities have caused or are likely to cause severe impacts, and cases to date suggest a pervasive problem.
Poor	Selected activities warrant widespread concern and action, as large-scale, persistent, and/or repeated severe impacts have occurred or are likely to occur.

Notes

Fagatele
Bay National Marine Sanctuary

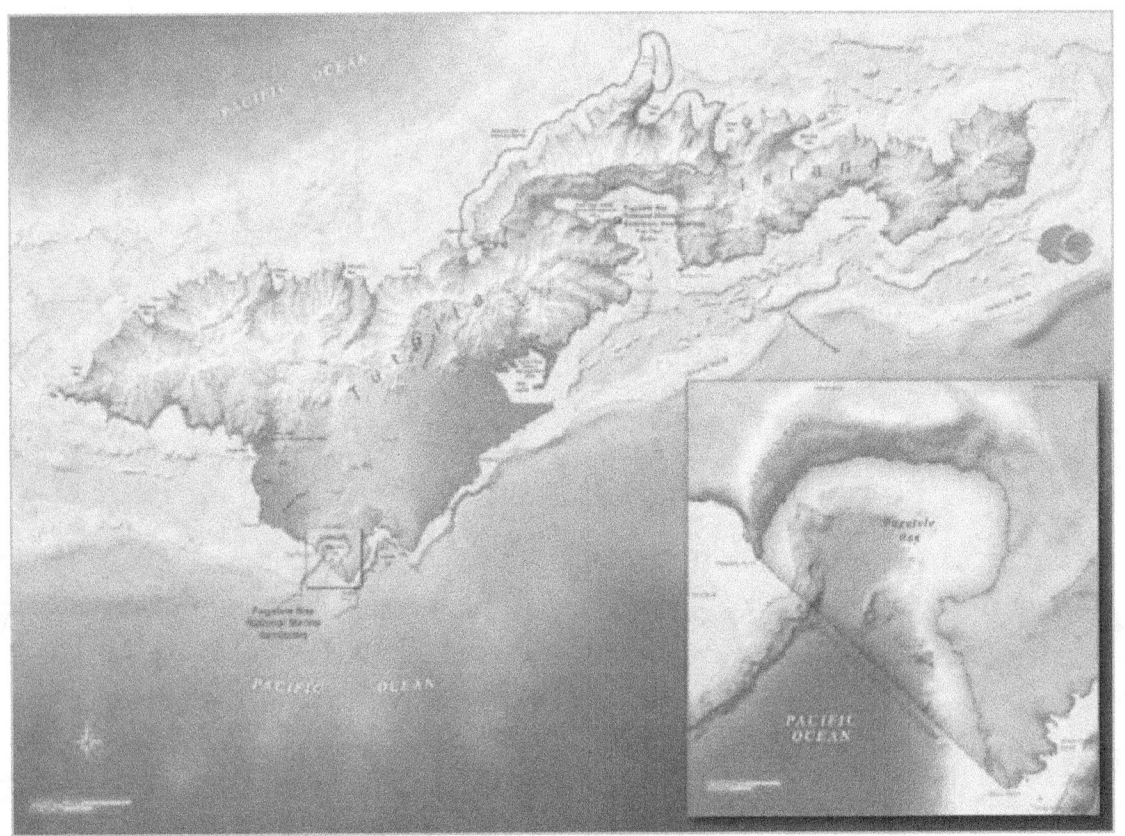

  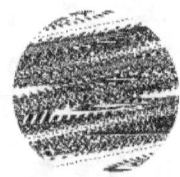 

NATIONAL MARINE
SANCTUARIES

www.ingramcontent.com/pod-product-compliance
Lightning Source LLC
Chambersburg PA
CBHW080344290526
45791CB00009BA/2724